W9-AVY-807

SOUL TRANSFORMATION

Engaging the Invisible Actor Within

by
SELINA MATTHEWS PHD

Foreword by
DENNIS SLATTERY PHD

Soul Transformation:
Engaging the Invisible Actor Within

Copyright © 2012 by Selina Matthews PhD

All rights reserved. No part of this book may be reproduced or transmitted in any form or by any means, electronic or mechanical including, photocopying, recording, or by any information storage and retrieval system, without written permission from the author, except for the inclusion of brief quotations in a review.

Disclaimer: I have been careful to assure that any patient identifying information has been sufficiently altered so that their confidentiality is protected. None of the patients discussed are active in my practice.

ISBN-10: 1467988553
EAN-13: 9781467988551

DEDICATION

To
Little Angel
And
To
Elizabeth Strahan
Whose Stars Shine Brightly
In
The
Great Beyond!

ACKNOWLEDGMENTS

My life's journey had been blessed with so many amazing healers, mentors, teachers, and friends and I am deeply grateful. The writing of this book was an intense experience and to everyone who listened to my story and provided me with support during the writing period, I thank you from the bottom of my heart.

I would like to express my great appreciation to several experts: Dennis Slattery PhD, who is always generous with his time, his extraordinary intellect, and his luminous wisdom—my gratitude is immeasurable and cosmic; Cindy Lindsay PhD, an extraordinary spiritual healer and teacher with whom I explore the ancient mysteries and depths of soul; the late Elizabeth Strahan, my Jungian analyst, for the tending of my soul; Johanna O'Flaherty PhD, for providing amazing feedback, as well as unwavering support and friendship; Kalea Chapman PhD, for providing feedback and helping me process some of my ideas; Sheila Forman PhD, for her friendship and brilliance; and Margaret Ryan, an incredibly gifted editor, to whom I am deeply indebted for encouraging me to find new ways to articulate my thoughts and ideas. I also have tremendous gratitude for Robin Mintzer PhD, and Dana Cook LCSW, who in their own unique ways provided me with support and friendship. A special thank-you to Katie McDonald for sharing her extraordinary story.

I am grateful and indebted to all of my patients especially those whose stories are illuminated in this book. You have made me grow and change my vision of what transformation is all about.

FOREWORD

Having served as advisor of Dr. Selina Matthews' dissertation committee as she completed her doctorate in Clinical Psychology at Pacifica Graduate Institute, I have watched her over the years deepen into a clinical therapist as well as broaden her reach from theory to praxis. Her first book, *The Transformational Power of Voice* (2010) which bore the fruits of her dissertation, had its genesis in her own loss of voice as an actress, followed by a long and arduous reclamation process in which she retrieved both her personal and professional power of utterance.

Now, in her second book, *Soul Transformation: Engaging the Inner Actor Within,* she once again returns to her own narrative as an actress to thicken the possibilities that: 1. We all resonate an inner actor in a life drama that is partly chosen, partly assigned, and 2. There are concrete effective behaviors we can all adapt as characters in our own fiction to more actively participate in shaping and thus transforming our life narrative. What both texts emphasize over all others is the absolute necessity of becoming more conscious and cognizant of who we are, what we feel, what we believe and what options are available to us in responding to the foregoing questions. In my own language, I would say that Selina is exploring the manner in which the lineaments of our narrative comprise our own personal myth. To enter the terrain or landscape of one's personal myth is to invite the presence of soul speech, which is another way of inquiring how we imagine our life narrative as an ordering principle to afford us a greater sense of conscious awareness.

In writing a book, one supreme act of courage is exposing one's own wounds, defects, shortcomings, as well as sufferings from personal experience. The danger, however, is always there that it can be done to excess. Selina knows intuitively when to let the reader in on her own pains, displacements and struggles to survive without becoming a victim of her own history. She does this at various intervals on her journey to make clear how "we can lead a split life, one through Contextual Factors, but still be not aligned with our soul journey." The invisible actor is the soul; the more we become aware of this actor's talents, biases, distortions, gifts, graces, the closer we can align ourselves to the story we are destined, though not by the same token fated, to live out. If individually we refuse the call to this narrative, it will not be lived out by anyone else. We have, as Selina intimates, a moral obligation to connect to our narrative and to give it voice and form in the world. To do so is to engage a fully authentic life, not a perfect one. Her premise throughout her study that combines both theory and praxis is that "the very nature of stories carry soul."

One of the most dramatic elements that hold Selina's exploration together in a complex unity, involves a process that she shares with C.G. Jung's work that he outlines in his last major text: *Mysterium Coniunctionis: An Inquiry into the Separation and Synthesis of Psychic Opposites in Alchemy* (1989: Vol. 14 of The Collected Works). In this synthetic text Jung suggests a process very akin to Selina's in his section entitled "The Conjunction." There Jung delineates "the production of the *caelum*," which is a "symbolic rite performed in the laboratory" in order to move the participant closer to "the celestial balsam or life principle." Now here is where Selina's work and Jung's own process find a common ground: in the realm of the drama as an action of soul, the role of the Invisible Actor, as Selina designates it. Jung suggests that within this process, which has as its aim to unite the conscious with the unconscious, if an individual simply remains passive to the drama, no transformation can occur, but instead only endless repetition of "what is enacted on the stage." Then, the cathartic effect will remain insignificant within this private theatre."

But, if the observer understands that his own drama is being performed on this inner stage, he cannot remain indifferent to the plot and its denouement. He will notice, as the actors appear one by one and the plot thickens, that they all have some purposeful relationship to his situation, that he is being addressed by the unconscious, and that it causes these fantasy images to appear before him. He therefore feels compelled, or is encouraged by his analyst, to take part in the play and, instead of just sitting in a theatre, really have it out with his alter ego. (CW 14: ¶ 706)

Selina's own work adds to this acute observation by Jung on the role of the actor and spectator, which can be the same person who explores the place of free will in this enterprise of the caelum. She believes unconditionally in the power of free will "as an ability to choose an action or course of actions in order to fulfill a personal desire for which you take responsibility both consciously and unconsciously."

Both in Selina's program outlined in detail through various stages, and in Jung's sense of the importance of the Inner Actor, one primary belief predominates. In Jung's language, "The process of coming to terms with the Other in us is well worth while, because in this way we get to know aspects of our nature which we would not allow anybody else to show us and which we ourselves would never have admitted" (par.¶ 706).

Our narratives are negotiable, our roles as actors optional, our participation freely chosen, not mandated. While Selina makes clear that in the "Soul Transformation Blueprint" the roles we are asked or demanded or coerced into or freely choose to play is one of seven realms in the process of transformation, many of the other terms are subsumed in the drama of becoming. Underlying both Jung's and Selina's vision is that of a whole life, not perfect but nonetheless complete in crucial ways. We are all, it appears, fictions, fabrications, fables, not in the sense of lies or untruths, but in the more imaginal sense that we are crafted stories with a plot that the adventure of life allows us to observe and to act in at the same instant. Selina's book will go a long way in leading the reader into this enchanted realm of story. Sign on for the journey; it will be a grand awakening on center stage!

Dennis Patrick Slattery, Ph.D.
23 December 2011
Author of: *The Wounded Body: Remembering the Markings of Flesh* and *Day-to-Day Dante: Exploring Personal Myth Through The Divine Comedy.*
www.dennispslattery.com

TABLE OF CONTENTS

PART 3 SOUL TRANSCENDENCE

PART I
THE SOUL

CHAPTER 1

INTRODUCTION

As I walked down the curved path toward my PhD class I noticed a glorious rainbow over the Joseph Campbell Library and thought what a good omen to begin the day. I was very excited because the class lecture was going to be taught by two professors whom I admire, one a Jungian analyst and the other a Freudian psychoanalyst. I respected both men for their clinical acumen and their commitment to teaching psychology.

Our class was not what you would call touchy feely like some of the other classes we had often heard about. Nope! We were the problem class that comes together at rare intervals, about every ten years or so. Our class was so difficult and complicated that we had to have group therapy sessions before class even started to relieve the anger and tension that was brewing and spewing in the room. We were an unusual bunch of characters with strong personalities who for a short period of time came together for one common purpose—to complete our PhDs in Clinical Psychology.

This morning lecture began in a lively manner with difficult clinical questions being addressed to both professors. It was fascinating to hear their approaches to the same question as both men were brilliant and clinically savvy. The battery of questions continued until one of the more exuberant students asked the question "Do you think that we are working with soul in our clinical work?" One professor said in a strong voice "Absolutely!" while the other one interjected "Absolutely *not!*" The room went silent for a moment and then when everyone caught their breath chaos ensued with the conflicting positions.

I was still caught in stun mode as the rest of the class made an attempt to move forward. The *absolutely not* hit a deep chord within me and I could hardly contain the rage and anger that were bubbling from deep within. All of a sudden the chord now taut snapped and catapulted me out of the room. I needed some air! I needed to breathe! I retreated to the Rose Garden and sat there. As I sat down I remembered a spiritual teacher telling me to look at an object of beauty to calm the mind when things get intense. So I sat there on the lawn communing with a luscious peach rose until I my mind settled. Why was I so angry? Well, it is my understanding that the soul is the driving force in our life because without it we could not exist—it is our hard drive. It is the *Who am I?* which holds the key to the ancient question *What is my purpose in life?* What got me so fired up was the notion of ignoring soul in our clinical work when it is the essence of who we are. Eventually I calmed down and went back to class.

Even though my body was in class, my mind was in a philosophical discussion about soul. I know that most people believe that there is a soul within them, but who, how and why it got there remains a mystery. When asked to define soul, very few people can because it is a difficult concept with which to grapple. Try defining it yourself and see what you come up with. Indeed religious leaders, philosophers and scholars have been wrestling with this dilemma for centuries. Some traditions have definitions and images of soul, whereas others consider it to be undefinable. Most of us can agree that within the flesh, blood and bones of human existence there is something eternal, ephemeral and intangible that connects them to the cosmos—something I now call the *Invisible Actor* within.

Many years have passed since that class and I have been working as a clinical psychologist for some time. I have had the opportunity to ponder and discus the matter of soul with many of my colleagues and clients who were interested in delving into that part of their psyche . . . always a fascinating discussion. However in the writing of this book I needed to find an accessible way to talk about soul so we could all be on the same page, so to speak.

I believe that soul and spirit are indelibly interwoven into the fabric of human existence. Historically I find it fascinating that the word *soul* was first recorded in Old English in 971, and was referred to as the spirit of a person who was dead. Nearly thirty years later the word *soul* was expanded to include the embodied spirit of a living person. The word *spirit* emerged much later around 1250 and was considered to be the breath of life, an animating principle in both human and animal.

Even though *soul* and *spirit* are essentially undefinable, I want to provide an imaginal way of experiencing them. I imagine the soul to be part of the spirit that lives in the body that is comprised of hues of color, texture, images, and impressions of our lived human experience as well as our inherent potentiality and destiny. Soul is eternal and it is from this perspective that I imagine it to contain imprinted energies from other lifetimes.

Spirit, on the other hand, is the part of soul that is connected with the divine light and breath of the cosmos. Spirit has a proclivity toward expansion and universality, whereas soul has an engagement with humanity and life experience. Soul is embodied whereas spirit is disembodied. Both aspects are essential: spirit provides the cosmic breath of life to enliven the flesh, while the soul embodies the eternal flame within the flesh, blood and bones of human existence. Philosophers and mystics have contemplated: Does the soul live in the body or does the body live in the soul? You decide. Clearly, the dance of spirit and soul is intimately engaged until death do them part or death do them unite in the cosmic realms. Some traditions do not separate the processes of soul from spirit, but experience the engagement of these two energies as soul.

Even though we all come into the world with soul very few of us are in relationship with our soul, know our soul purpose, or even understand how to connect with our soul energy. In fact most psychological theorists do not address soul at all. Nevertheless, philosophers and depth psychologists have been bridging this gap and have been educating humanity about soul and spirit for quite some time. Carl Jung believed that the soul was the true focus of psychology and many of his contemporaries, each in their own unique way, such as, Edward Edinger, James Hillman, Thomas Moore, Robert Romanyshn, and Lionel Corbett, to name a few, have followed in this tradition.

Soul Transformation: Engaging the Invisible Actor Within is a depth psychological book that examines the engagement of soul in the human experience through a nonlinear blending of philosophical, psychological, and soul transformational approaches that allow the reader a unique interpretation of his or her reality. This book engages an experiential framework that fosters greater understandings of those existential questions we all face sometimes in our lives: *Who am I?* and *What is my soul purpose?* The structure of this book is set within a five-stage model of Soul Transformation. The five Soul Transformation stages are:

1. Awakening of soul.

2. Soul stirrings.

3. Soul engagements.

4. Deconstructing illusions.

5. Continual soul engagement.

Part I, "The Soul," addresses the first three stages of Soul Transformation. *Awakening of Soul* is the first stage of the soul journey in the human realm, although we are not yet conscious enough to engage its presence. Once the soul awakens into human form, it enters into the trance of illusion—the veils that cover the soul after the birth experience. I term these veils *contextual factors,* and they have both *personal* and *impersonal* significance for one's life. It is extraordinarily important to acknowledge and be conscious of these factors because they become the software operating system that creates your world-view.

In *Soul Stirrings*, the second stage, the soul, the Invisible Actor within, reawakens. I believe this to be a universal experience typically occurring in our adulthood years, from the age of around eighteen through our thirties. Once stirred, the Invisible Actor gently moves us toward change if we allow it. Soul stirrings, in essence, give us a glimpse of how, what, where, and why we become who we are. Even though theses stirrings may create suffering to some extent, and we may not want to deal with the feelings they create, we would remain unconscious without them. Life is never linear. Rather it is labyrinthian in nature, and it is our stirrings that lead us more deeply into our fully "ensouled" selves. Many examples of soul stirrings will be presented to catalyze your understanding of the process.

Soul Engagements, the third stage, comprises magical moments of unordinary experience that take us out of our mundane reality into the divine realms—numinous, miraculous, and spiritual experiences reign prominently in this stage. These experiences may be expected, unexpected, or come at chosen moments. Such divine engagements have the ability to alter the psychological development of a human being, and they need to be honored and addressed. Examples of soul engagements will be presented along with some practical ways to engage with soul.

Part II, "How to Deconstruct Your Illusions," includes *Deconstructing Illusions,* the fourth stage, comprising techniques that can assist you with peeling off the layers of contextual factors that inhibit your movement. This is the process of differentiating what we thought our reality was verses what it actually *is*, a sometimes painful process of self-discovery. The purpose of this stage is to move you closer to the Invisible Actor within. Also addressed in this section is the importance of mentorship and how it facilitates the deconstruction process.

Since stage four is multilayered, I have included philosophical, psychological, and soul perspectives to set the stage and provide a frame of reference. The goal of this section of the book is to give you multifaceted ways of thinking about your life as well as to provide you with a deeper understanding of the change and soul transformation process so that you could make better choices. The philosophical reflections in this section include a consideration of reality verses illusion and our use of free will in the choices we make. Psychological approaches include the spectrum of change involved in soul transformation as well as the compensation factor that shapes the illusions we hold. The three Soul Transformation approaches in this section include the Trinity Model, the Soul Transformation Process, and the Soul Transformation Blueprint—each of which offers a unique way to engage, catalyze, and live the soul transformation process.

More specifically, *The Trinity Model* explores the Healthy, Shadow, and Divine Sides of life in an easy-to-understand manner that allows you to put your life into perspective so that you can analyze your journey and illuminate aspects that were previously invisible. You will learn more about yourself, the roles that you play, and the reasons you may have made the choices that you did.

The *Soul Transformation Process* provides a five-stage guided meditation so that you can shift your stance and recreate the vision of your future and your life from a soul perspective.

The *Soul Transformation Blueprint,* a seven-stage template, integrates the concepts that are discussed throughout the book enabling you to addresses four important questions: *Who am I? Where am I in life? Where am I going? What is my soul purpose?* This template is an active process allowing you to analyze your life through the roles you engage in and helps you to begin to understand your own entrapments, which may have begun in your family of origin. In the process, you discover pathways to move out from them so that you can live with authenticity the life you were destined to live.

Part III, "The Transcendent Soul" describes the fifth stage, *Continual Soul Engagement* which has the amazing aspirational goal of transcendence and enlightenment. No differentiation or separation is needed here because it is the place of recognizing our essential oneness with the universe. In this final stage of soul transformation the eternal flame of transcendent divinity is unwavering. However, very few of us actually reach this goal so holding it in our hearts and minds as a beacon keeps us moving in an authentic soul-centered direction.

This book will help you to revision your life and move you toward a soul-centered perspective that values integrity, dignity, authenticity, and purpose. It will help you to get closer to finding out the existential answers to those eternal questions: *Who am I?* and *What is my soul purpose?* In the process you will increase your level of consciousness and free yourself from the invisible constraints, the shackles that bind you. You will learn how to transform your life in a way that is more aligned with the Invisible Actor within.

CHAPTER 2

AWAKENING OF SOUL

The birth of a baby is one of the most exciting and precious experiences in the human realm. The transformation from a fetus immersed in the mother's amniotic fluid into human form breathing universal air is nothing short of miraculous. The first and most precious breath that the baby takes ignites the first stage of Soul Transformation, the *Awakening of Soul* into the human realm.

At birth the soul awakens and enters into what has been called for centuries, the trance of illusion, the veils that cover the soul at birth. As I understand it, the veils comprise the conscious and unconscious projections and illusions of family, friends, culture, community, career, religion, geographic location, environment, political milieu, and government that the life is born into, which I refer to as the *impersonal* set of contextual factors that shape our earth experience. At birth our family, friends, culture and sometimes religion surround us with preset ideas about who they want us to become, the schools they want us to attend, the professions they want us to have, and the places they want us to live. All these ideas and perspectives over time become extraordinarily powerful grids of energies and coordinates of experience that begin working their way into our psyche and body via osmosis beginning at birth. From birth through early adult life we are a sponge to these energetic patterns, projections and illusions. Sometimes these perspectives are limiting and other times they are expansive, depending on the family. Some of them may be soul-centered, but most are not. From birth and onward they are the veils that cover our soul. And yet as the baby grows and develops he or she will encounter many intense life experiences that will also affect his or her psychological development and skew his or her worldview. These experiences form the second *personal* set of contextual factors.

To clarify, the *contextual factors* comprise the impersonal and personal conditions of our life. The *impersonal* contextual factors influence us from birth onward and include the conscious and unconscious projections and illusions of family, friends, culture, community, career, religion, geographic location, environment, political milieu, and government. The *personal* contextual factors include an individual's personal life experiences that have influenced them in some manner. Both sets of these contextual factors are salient because they shape our way of approaching and interpreting life. These contextual factors must be taken seriously because they have lifelong consequences. Their invisible influence lives within every one of us. We don't even know they exist, just like a fish doesn't know that it is in water, that is, until someone pulls it out. *Consciousness is always a wake-up call.*

We all learn about the impersonal contextual factors through the process of modeling, absorption, osmosis, self-discovery, innate predispositions, instincts, and personal experiences. Most of the everyday movements, postures, gestures, manners, mannerisms, voice, and rituals that we perform have been around prior to our birth. We copy them because we have seen them and heard them a thousands of times during our lifetime and we are trying to fit in. Some of them are symbolic and ritualized whereas others are indoctrinated or trained. All of them will continue to be performed unconsciously without any type of analysis, unless we make a choice to bring them into our personal consciousness. Even our everyday emotions, such as the way that we laugh or cry, can be learned from our contextual factors in some manner. How many people do you know that laugh like their mother or father? Over time the appropriateness or unsuitableness of all these learned emotions and body languages becomes a fixed part of our identity, many of which we may not even be aware of. Also our personal contextual factors reign prominently because they color our perspective; for example, if you were molested or raped, your worldview would be very different from someone who had a healthy, positive upbringing with out any type of traumatic experience.

Existing within every family is that ever-present Invisible Actor that allows each family member to have his or her own distinct soul journey and potentiality, which is for each to discover alone. The art of personal distinction comes from knowing your own soul journey and separating it from your family members. For some people the soul journey process is very subtle and easy, whereas others find it is visibly difficult and complicated because of psychological enmeshment and dysfunction.

If soul is your hard drive, then I would like you to imagine these contextual factors as the software operating systems that we all have etched within our flesh from birth onward. These software programs are intimately connected to our psychological and spiritual process because it is the way we run our life. Although we may never really understand all the intricacies of our contextual factors, we can bring consciousness to them and see how they work in our life and make the appropriate choices in the way we want to live.

Initially the contextual factors provide us with the *Who am I?,* beginning in the womb and then continuing throughout life. They become our way of framing life, our phenomenology, our lived experience. Later on our personal life experiences adds to our psychological makeup. Nevertheless, we can be trapped by any of these contextual energies unless we find a way out from them, as I will demonstrate in later chapters.

Our Contextual Factors

Contextual factors come with a cast of characters, plot, and setting. Initially the contextual factors set up our likes, dislikes, values, morals, and relational abilities. They are the *Who, What, When, Where*, and *How*, of who we are or who we think we are. In the beginning of our life journey we are not cognizant of our soul perspective or purpose. However as we grow older and experience life, questions such as *Who Am I?* can raise a lot of inner inquiry. As you move through the life span and are exposed to different experiences you might have asked yourself: "Am I just the sum total of my contextual factors, or is there more to me than that?" And the answer is *yes*—there is more to you. But before you consider the soul level, you must know your story and the contextual factors that surround you because they have assisted in forming who you have become. I believe that writing down our stories and sharing them with another person is really important. In the process we learn about ourselves, our life choices, our limitations, and growth potentialities. It is from this perspective that I share with you my personal story and contextual history.

My *Impersonal* Contextual Factors

I was born Selene Jo Oneschuk in a small farming community in the great, vast, Canadian prairies. The town, Two Hills, located one hundred miles north of the nearest city, had a population of nine hundred people. Most of the people who lived there were of Ukrainian, Polish, or Romanian decent. The cultural diversity of this area included a Hutterite settlement and a Native American Indian Reserve, both located within a twenty-mile radius of the town. Farming, along with cattle and pig ranching, were the primary business ventures. My father was a farmer who planted wheat, oats, and barley, and worked at the local chemical plant. I guess that makes me a *small-town farm girl*.

Being Ukrainian is my birthright, a setup prior to my birth. It made me culturally who I am and it came with its own food, music and dance. The town I was born in gave me community, rules, education and a perspective from which to experience life. My parents gave me their genetic lineage, morals, values, and religious beliefs. I was baptized in the Ukrainian Greek Orthodox church. Astrology gave me the Sagittarian planetary sign and celestial imprint. I was the first-born child, a trailblazer, with two brothers, Douglas and Cameron, born after me.

The *Who am I?* when I was born and the *Who am I?* now have very different answers. The *small-town farm girl* would have never have imagined that she would be living in a big cosmopolitan city, or even that she would be a clinical psychologist—in fact she didn't even know what that was until she was an adult. However, life presented me with challenging adventures and even though the journey was at times tumultuous, I was able to really transform my life. The *small-town farm girl* still lives within my psychic flesh and I honor her. She is part of me and will never leave me. She connects me with the earth and keeps me grounded and I embrace her presence deep within.

My *Personal* Contextual Factors

After my birth my parents both worked so that they could create a life that was different from the life into which they were born. My grandmother, "Baba," came to live with us so that she could care for me while my parents went to their respective jobs. I adored Baba and treasured every moment with her. Around the age of five, she was removed from the family home, a story that I address in a later chapter. Her abrupt departure when I was just five years old changed my reality and moved me into another mode . . . survival!

Growing up in this small town I did the regular things that kids do: piano lessons, baseball, Ukrainian dancing, and figure skating lessons, to name a few. However, when I was about twelve years old my parents purchased a dry goods store as a way to increase their income and to own their own business. It was my responsibility to work there every day after school and on weekends as well as to keep up with my grades. My reality changed once again with all the added pressure of working in this business.

As a young teenager I was quite popular and began dating around the age of fourteen. I had very strict curfews and boundaries enforced by my parents. Coming home after a date was never pleasant—in fact, it was downright awful. As I would go up the stairs towards my room, my mother would be sitting at the kitchen table waiting for me so that she could smell my breath to see if I was smoking or drinking. I felt violated with this weekly ritual. And like any teenager, I was not perfect and broke the rules at times. I masked my indiscretions by chewing a lot of gum. Sometimes I was caught, other times not. Around this time period I began having problems at school and my grades dropped. My parents thought it might be a good idea for me to complete my grade 12 in Edmonton, away from the influence of some of my friends. So when I was sixteen years old, I moved to Edmonton. This geographical move, one hundred miles from Two Hills, along with change in home life, friends, school, and community was both a frightening and elating experience because I left my family behind to finish my high school education at a better school so I could forge ahead in my life. I was actually surprised that my parents let me leave their strict supervision. In Edmonton I had my own little apartment one block away from school so it was easy to get there. Victoria Composite High School was large, twenty times larger than the school that I went to in Two Hills. I liked the new school academically, but I was different from the other kids—I did not look like or dress like them and they made sure I knew that by making fun of me. They made me feel like a freak. They made me ashamed of who I was—a small town farm girl with corny-looking clothes. My self-confidence plummeted and I wanted only two things, to hide who I was, and try to find a way to fit in.

Modeling became the answer—it saved me. I talked my parents into letting me take the classes and not only did I create a supportive community of friends, teachers, and mentors, I was taught how to walk, sit, stand, dress, and how put on makeup. It was my version of Finishing School that assisted in helping me develop a new persona, one that saved me from further humiliation for which I was truly grateful. My life at seventeen was transforming and I was making choices for my future as well as adapting to my new environment simultaneously. My reality was changing!

My move to Edmonton along with the modeling classes really transformed the direction of my life and separated me from a lot of the contextual factors into which I was born. I made new friends, had new mentors, and made life choices that I never would have previously imagined. I am grateful that I was grounded enough to enjoy my new found freedoms.

Exploring Your Contextual Factors

Exploring your contextual factors is an extraordinarily important exercise. Begin with journaling about your life story, starting with the *impersonal* contextual factors of your birth and then follow with any *personal* contextual factors that were important, life-altering experiences, good or bad. Writing them down can be a cathartic experience that helps you connect to a deeper part of your personal myth—because you indeed are a character and participant in your life. Concretizing your story through writing only deepens your understanding of what happened! In the process you may even learn something about yourself. I know I did.

CHAPTER 3

SOUL STIRRINGS

oul Stirrings, the second stage of soul transformation, embraces both the psychological and spiritual aspects of life. Here we focus on the spiritual. It is my understanding that anytime from the age of around eighteen though our thirties there is a soul stirring process that occurs even though we may not even be cognizant of it. During these soul stirrings we contemplate our life choices to see if we are going in the direction that we wanted to go and for many of us this process is a shocking wakeup call. What we thought was going to happen didn't and instead other things happened that we never imagined. It is a time when we realize, however dimly, that something is profoundly wrong and our life is not working. I believe the process begins after the age of eighteen because it isn't until then that we finish high school and focus on our career paths. Some individuals will choose college whereas others go directly to the work force: each path has different challenges. By the time we are in our twenties, a lot of things have happened to us that define us, shape us, and influence our future possibilities. We are considered to be full-blooded adults at this time, in careers, making money, and moving forward on the unrelenting treadmill of time. Yet at any time during this time frame something deep within us can stir, as we begin to assess our place in life, form our worldview, and begin to analyze our life—it is the hard drive activating itself. The timing for each individual stirring is unique and deeply personal.

Soul stirrings are part of the individuation process, in which we separate and differentiate ourselves from our surroundings—a concept that was initially developed by Carl Jung. Soul stirrings move us out from the shackles, our enmeshment with our family and culture, and into the direction of becoming unique human beings. Soul stirrings are the advancement of the psychological and spiritual aspects of a human being through to his or her fullest potential, allowing for an individual to embrace the world in a differentiated way. Birthdays and specific events are generally good markers that allow us to look back at a specific time and remember, where we came from and to now discern the flickering clues to where our soul stirrings are headed.

Soul stirrings allow us to begin the process of discovering our authentic self in the world. They make us sink into the depth of our pain to find our essence, so that we can connect with the *Invisible Actor,* the soul, that wants to emerge in our life. It walks alongside us, bringing a deep guiding presence to our life and is the only part that can really answer the deeper question of *Who am I?* The existential pondering of *Who am I?* is always influx as we move though the life span. The eternal flame can deepen to its fullest capacity only if we allow it so perhaps it would be better to say, *Who am I becoming?*

Recognizing Soul Stirrings

Soul stirrings are an internal wake-up call—a reawakening guided by the eternal flame within—making us aware that we are not moving toward our soul purpose. These stirring can lead to positive change and transformation but if the call for change is repressed it can lead to depression, despair, and addiction, to name but a few undesirable outcomes.

Calista, a twenty-seven-year-old casually dressed woman came into treatment for her depression. She was tired of trying every depression medication in the medical pharmacopeia because none of them had provided her with the magic bullet that she wanted. She told me that she was very unhappy about the way that her life was going: all of her friends had university degrees and were moving forward in their life and she was not. She had spent most of the time partying and trying to get her modeling career on track but was unable to earn a decent living. She was able to live this bohemian lifestyle because she was being supported or should I say enabled by her affluent parents. Nevertheless, she did end up in my office and was ready to do something about her debilitating depression . . . her soul was stirring.

In another case, Amora, now twenty-eight became aware of how unhappy she was when she was about twenty-two years old. Her depression was a slow-burning downward spiral into darkness. She couldn't really articulate why she was unhappy or what triggered it, but she knew that she wanted something different. At twenty-five she wanted to get away from her home situation so she moved in with her boyfriend, but that fantasy soon became a hard, cold, reality and the relationship lasted only ten months. Her illusions crashed up against the reality of her relationship and catalyzed her to seek therapy. She wanted to explore all of her options, because she no longer wanted to live with darkness and despair. She wanted more control of her life . . . her soul was stirring.

Zak a very attractive thirty-five-year-old man worked as a model in his early years but was no longer earning that juicy income. Five years ago he married a wealthy women, but after the first year the relationship was not what he thought it was going to be (illusions once again demolished by reality), so he began popping pills to deal with his unhappiness. When he showed up at my office he was taking fifteen Vicodin a day to numb himself from the emotional pain that he felt. He knew that if he stayed in his marriage he would die and he did not want to die . . . his soul was stirring.

The soul-stirring process for each individual is different in terms of timing and manner that it emerges depending on the contextual factors and personality of the individual. Understanding *your* story, and knowing when and why you got derailed, no matter what age you are deepens your understanding of self.

My Soul-Stirring Story

I remember celebrating my twenty-fifth birthday by going out to an amazing restaurant with my modeling agent, boyfriend, and some friends. We were all laughing and having a great time and then my boyfriend asked me to open an envelope. I was very excited . . . opened it . . . a *Sympathy Card* . . . Ha Ha Ha! Everyone laughed while I sat there totally stunned. I could not believe that he would give me such a card because he knew how upset I was to be turning a quarter of a century, and he knew what a big deal this birthday was. I could barely look at him across the table because my rage and anger were seeping out of every pore of my body. Even though it was hard to hide, I controlled my feelings and did not disrupt the evening. However, an internal storm was brewing!

Why was I so angry at becoming twenty-five years old? Well, my life was not going the way I imagined it would go and lots of bad things happened to me. Now to be fair, a lot of good things happened to me as well, but why is it that I focused on the bad?

My brother Douglas had died five years ago when he was just sixteen . . . a motorcycle accident. He was my best friend and I loved him deeply. I knew he was going to die when I saw him lying on the gurney at the hospital. I remember looking at him and watching him slowly turn his head away from me. Tears gushed from my eyes because I knew his fate, so I left the room and hid in the stairwell away from everyone, alone, until I got the fatal news.

The funeral was an open-casket ceremony at a church. Inside, carefully placed, were Doug's waxed remains for all to see. His soul, the eternal flame within had departed. That day I learned that a dead body is not the person, but it is the soul that makes the person. Doug did not look like himself, which was devastating for me to face. He was embodied one day and then disembodied the next. The reality I once knew was forever changed and I remember thinking: *Did Doug really know how much I loved him?* That day I learned an important lesson—life is precious, delicate, and ephemeral, and we need to honor it more than we do. As I walked by my beloved brother for the last time I knew I would never have the opportunity to kiss him, and I wanted that memory. I gently placed my hand on his cold forehead and poured my heart into the last kiss that I gave him . . . my heart was breaking. I remember thinking, *Will I ever get through this?*

The last year in Edmonton was so phenomenal for me in a positive way when I was crowned Miss Edmonton—an honor because I never imagined that the small town farm girl would ever win. No one else imagined it either because everyone was dumbfounded when my name was announced as the winner. I clearly remember my parents telling me that the judges must have made a mistake to have chosen me.

The winner of the Miss Edmonton beauty pageant was given the honor of competing for the title of Miss Canada, a national event held in Toronto. It was a thrilling experience to go there and meet all the beautiful young women representing every province in Canada. There were so many exciting doorways to my future opening, yet another doorway was closing, the finality of life. Two days after Doug's funeral, I was to appear on television to give up my crown as Miss Edmonton to the new beauty pageant winner. With the help and support of a lot of people including the modeling agency with which I was affiliated, I fulfilled my duty and gave up my crown with grace and simplicity. My brother Douglas was going to be my date that night and rented a white tuxedo to escort me to the function—it was the suit in which he was buried.

In one year I experienced the stark polarities of human emotion—I went from an amazing life-expanding situation to a devastating life-shattering situation. My life was undeniably altered by both experiences. After Doug's death, shock, depression, and despair followed me everywhere—they were my newfound companions. I was not functional and could not find solace anywhere so my father insisted that I go back to university to try and complete my term. I tried to tell him what was happening to me emotionally, but he just didn't understand. So I lied about going to school and I drove to the university parking lot and stared at nothing. I was paralyzed with grief—months passed by.

I was clinically depressed and could not talk to anyone. My family considered it shameful to tell anyone your problems, so I didn't. I certainly needed help though I was acting like a zombie, completely nonfunctional. I wish that someone had taken me to a psychologist to help me deal with my grief and sadness but I did not know that these kinds of people existed. I didn't even know it was okay to get help.

The days and months of grieving blurred into a stormy cloud of pain that followed me everywhere. The family attempted to pull together, but never really did. Everything changed and everything was different. Doug was positioned to work in and eventually take over the new family business a hotel now located in Edmonton, but he was dead. My eleven year-old brother Cameron and I were left to carry on. I felt that I had to pull my weight at the family business now—it was not my dream but I worked with my family now and my reality changed once again.

Six months or so after Doug's death, my friends dragged me to a party and I met a guy, older than the guys I had dated before. The relationship progressed very quickly because I was lonely, I missed my brother, and this guy offered me an exciting possibility. I fell fast in love. All was going well until my parents found out that I was having premarital sex. Well, our value systems collided—I could not believe their response to me given that I was now an adult. One cold, rainy evening my parents hauled me into the business office, slammed the door, and shamed me for disgracing the family. They belittled me, calling me everything from a street-walker to a whore, so I did what they demanded and got married. Marriage became a way out of the insanity I was living in. It was a beautiful wedding with Baked Alaska flaming at every table. The marriage lasted maybe two months—it had no chance. It was just another failure that my family never let me forget. This failed marriage was now layered on top of the loss of my brother, along with everything else that lurked beneath these two events. The shame and depression that I was living with were unbearable . . . I hid from life for the next two years and went nowhere.

Who am I at twenty-five? I have already been married, divorced, and have lived through the tragic death of my beloved brother. I have experienced many things in life and know a lot about pain, grief, shame, and emptiness. The life that I once imagined of being happily married with two children and living in suburbia in a house with a white picket fence, has not happened. The knight in shining armor that was supposed to save me, hasn't. Where did I go wrong?

The Hero and Heroine's Journey

Every story has a real set of events, some of which we can control, while others we have no control over, except in how we respond to the situation. If we see ourselves only as part of the contextual factors of our lineage, we are then pre-programmed into a certain type of response. In other words, there is no choice—the contextual factors makes the choice for us and in some way they define our life. Some families and cultures have tools to deal with life-altering events, whereas others do not. If there are no transformative tools available, depression, denial, and darkness will prevail unless outside help is offered

Life provides us with many lessons but when we make decisions based on our family situation and contextual factors, those decisions are imbued with illusions and projections that may not be aligned with our specific soul journey. For example, they may push us to grow in a manner that we may not have chosen or wanted, like my brief marriage. Unfortunately, you will always have to own the consequence of your decision, whether you choose it or it is chosen for you. Your family, culture, and society at large does not suffer the same consequence.

Soul stirrings signify the beginning of the hero and heroine's journey, an archetypal template for the human capacity to experience transformation. The hero's transformative adventure begins when an individual who is unsatisfied or failing in some manner with his or her ordinary life experience goes on an adventure beyond the ordinary to recover what was lost. Joseph Campbell refers to this as the call to adventure that signifies that destiny has summoned the hero and transferred his or her spiritual center of gravity from within the pale of society to a zone unknown. It is a perilous journey to unknown destinations as well as explorations of the dark and shadow aspects that lurk in both the inner and outer worlds. It is the cycle of life and death, through themes of redemption and salvation, that entails the recovery of the eternal flame that was lost or dimmed through one's life experience. Some journeys are chosen whereas others just happen, like disasters, geographical moves, and untimely deaths, to name a few.

Soul stirring adventures require that you leave your comfort zone and immerse yourself in the transmuting fires of life to encounter the capacity of your mettle. Transformation occurs when you lose your self to a higher self, the spiritual and divine sides of life. The hero's journey is a heroic transformation of consciousness because it honors a force bigger than oneself—it is *soul transformation*. Anyone can engage in soul transformation if they follow the stirrings of the Invisible Actor within.

Exploring Your Soul Stirrings

Soul stirrings are wakeup calls that bring forth the message that something is not quite right in your life. Exploring your soul-stirring story by journaling deepens your understanding of what has happened to you. It is exciting to rediscover the soul-stirring event or events that motivated you toward change and transformation. If an event or person stopped you from making a change, also write down what happened, because all these moments are crucial for analyzing your life journey. Soul stirrings ignite your heroic journey, the journey that takes you to the depths of your eternal flame, the Invisible Actor within. Reclaiming your journey and sharing your story has tremendous cathartic merit. I encourage you to discover more about yourself as you engage the Invisible Actor within.

CHAPTER 4

SOUL ENGAGEMENT

Soul Engagement is the third stage of soul transformation. It usually occurs after the soul-stirring process has been set in motion. Soul Engagement is all about the alignment of the divine and spiritual energies that exist within your flesh, blood, and bones with those that exist in the cosmos—an internal and external cosmic experience. It is a process that usually begins with an *un*ordinary experience that allows for movement in an unknown or unfamiliar direction and acts as a catalyst for uniting inner and outer divinity. These unordinary embodied experiences are magical moments that catapult us out of our mundane reality and transport us into the divinity that is universal.

Raina came into therapy to discuss her husband's philandering, which had gone on for years. She felt she couldn't leave him until the kids had completed high school and now that time had come. Just as she was getting ready to leave her marriage, she was diagnosed with breast cancer and had to have a mastectomy. She was devastated. The night before the surgery she had this vision:

I was lying in the room by myself. Everybody had gone home. My surgery was scheduled for seven o'clock the next morning. I was very scared. As I lay there, I reminisced about my life and the choices I had made and wondered if the cancer was indirectly caused by my husband. Tears began to pour out of my eyes and then my body began to shake and I thought that maybe I was dying. And then I saw this intense ray of light that was so strong and powerful that it nearly took my breath away. Through the light, I saw an emerging vision . . . it was GOD. He was both real and unreal. His presence came towards me and placed his hand on my forehead and told me that everything was going to be okay. Then he told me that it was not my time to die and that I still had work that I needed to accomplish. And then he vanished. I was in shock!

Raina was afraid to tell anyone about this experience because she didn't want people to think that she was crazy. After the surgery, which was successful, her relationship with God deepened and she felt a renewed purpose to her life. She ended her marriage and went back to school to get a degree to enable her to work with emotionally disturbed children, something she had always wanted to do. She is now passionate about her life, her children, and new career.

Patients have discussed many profound, unordinary experiences in therapy. It is my understanding that these experiences consciously or unconsciously manifest and influence us toward our authentic soul journey. After encountering these divine experiences, there is a tremendous potentiality for transformation to occur on multiple levels of the human experience. For example, we may leave the influence of our contextual factors to discover the deeper parts of our authentic self, the perilous part of our soul journey.

Soul engagement alters our psychological framework and deepens the pilgrimage of the hero and heroine. It is here that we encounter unknown and unexplored internal and external landscapes in order to experience the depths of our *self* and connect to the Invisible Actor within that has now enlivened, flickering its bright, shiny, eternal flame to illuminate our path.

In order for soul engagement to occur, three processes must be in place. First, you must have an ability to access soul energy; second, you must be available and open to having divine experiences; and third, you must allow the experience to unfold organically. Soul engagement allows for spiritual expansion both internally and externally because it is a divine intervention that moves you out of your contextual factors and aligns the divine inner part of you with cosmic divinity. During these times the Invisible Actor is realigning you with your potential and soul destiny.

In this third phase of life's theatre, the stage is set, the atmosphere is created, choices are made, and events happen, some organically, some created. Rebecca shared with me her story where she set the stage and received the unexpected:

> When I got married, my mother and both grandmothers were long gone. I planned our wedding myself with no "borrowed, new or blue" cultural artifacts. I decided to do something outside the bounds of my upbringing— something that neither mother nor grandmothers did. I went to the local Mikvah, the Jewish ritual bath before our wedding. I made this choice out of a need and a sense that I might be able to connect to the generations of Jewish women who came before me. Even though my mother and grandmother did not partake, the generations ahead of them certainly had.
>
> My friend, who was a religious Jewish woman, set it up. I followed the rules ahead of time. I felt nervous and out of place when I entered the chamber. As I began my emersion I had an experience that I'd never had before. It was so out of my realm that I had no words for it when I left. As the emersion proceeded I experienced an opening above me. There was a radiant illumination of light shining down on me. This light seemed to me at

the time, an invitation. "Talk to me" it seemed to mean. I spontaneously started to pray, pray from my soul—pray for real. This illumination shocked me, shook me, and scared me.

I got up out of the water, glanced meekly at the attendant who had been instructing me, and walked into the outer room to dress. When I came out of the dressing room, a gaggle of women shouted joyously and threw candy at me, apparently a ritual as well. I believe that what happened was real to this day. It was a singular moment, and I've never had any like it again. I was heard.

Rebecca went to the Mikvah to participate in a sacred ritual that was part of her religious tradition. She wanted to connect to her ancestral heritage through this ceremonial act, but what happened was an unordinary divine experience that deepened her connection to God and left her feeling incredibly peaceful.

When soul engagement occurs, you may feel strange, unfamiliar, or even chaotic, but underlying this embodied experience is an internal knowing, a divinity that moves you forward. Even though this third stage happens anytime from roughly eighteen through the thirties, it is never too late for anyone to experience this stage, as long as they create and engage in the architecture that supports it. For some exceptional individuals these soul experiences occur early in their life, though it is rare.

I explore three types of soul engagements: numinous, spiritual, and miraculous, providing examples of each. I imagine these types of soul engagement as a spectrum of experience that moves increasingly toward different levels of complexity and unfoldment.

Numinous Experiences

Numinous experiences are unplanned, unordinary events that erupt out of the body and soul of an individual without conscious warning as illustrated by Rina and Rebecca's stories. These unusual experiences exude a quality of *tremendous mystery* that resonates in divine nature. These types of experiences are thought to happen to anywhere from 30 to 50 percent of the population and can manifest in many forms—through dreams, visions, inner voices, and body experiences. They have been written about for centuries in classic texts such as the *Bible* and Dante's *Divine Comedy*, to name but two. A biblical example of the numinous is God appearing to Job from a whirlwind, and in *Paradisio*, Dante experiences his heart's desire spoken through the voice of an eagle. Historically, numinous experiences have been documented in the lives of Socrates, Joan of Arc, St. John of the Cross, and more recently Mother Theresa, who experienced an inner voice tell her to leave her cloistered life to work among the throngs with the poorest of the poor. Other examples of numinous experiences, including my own, will be presented.

Chalice, a beautiful thirty-four-year-old African American women, whose case I discuss in a Chapter Five, recounted an unexpected numinous experience that she had one weekend:

> It was about 7 p.m. when I decided to go for a walk. After I'd walked about a block, I suddenly felt this intense pang of hunger, followed by the thought that that I was going to lose control of my bowels. I immediately became dizzy, hot, and began sweating profusely. I thought that I'd better go home because something was not right. All of a sudden I felt like I was thrown to the ground, couldn't speak, couldn't move, and all I could do is look up at the sky. I thought that maybe I was dying, so I decided to accept my fate. A moment later the intensity of the night sky became magnified. The colors of the trees and the other objects in my periphery were also exaggerated. I looked up and noticed that the sky was falling and instantly became aware of this bright star coming toward me, trying to connect with me. It was like the star was directly communicating with me, and I didn't know why, or what it was trying to tell me.

After the experience subsided Chalice was speechless and motionless on the grass until she was able to gather herself and walk home. She did not know what had happened to her when she recounted this event to me in a therapy session, and she referred to it as a bizarre experience. I explained to her the concept of the numinous as well as the three distinct phases that occur.

The first phase of a numinous experience is the *Deconstruction Phase*, in which the body breaks down in some manner, as Chalice experienced when she became suddenly sick, dizzy, sweating, and feeling like she was losing control of her bowels. In the second phase, the *Acceptance Phase,* Chalice thinks she is dying and decides to accept her fate. A numinous experience will not occur if you fight the process and do not accept the deconstruction that is happening to you at that particular moment. Accepting the deconstruction enables you to receive the third phase, which presents itself when the suffering has ended. The third phase, the *Gift Phase,* is the awakening of a new aspect of your spiritual side.

After this numinous experience subsided, Chalice felt that a part of her that she'd never had access to was ignited. Everything in her life had changed—it was both profound and subtle. She felt that the experience was an initiation to open her up to new levels of spirituality. She was clearly engaged in the third phase of soul engagement. I told her that Carl Jung proclaimed that just one numinous experience was worth years of psychotherapy. She was elated to hear that! In an interesting synchronicity, the same day that this numinous experience occurred, Chalice had begun a Hindu mantra practice. Was this synchronicity, fate, or the Invisible Actor at play? Or all three.

Since numinous experiences come unexpectedly and without notice, we can't focus on creating them—we can't *will* them to happen—but we can focus on our spiritual practices. The spiritual quest is to get beyond the self into the truth of all things—the land of the unknown. In Chalice's case she was now deeply immersed in stage three of soul transformation as well as her own heroine's journey. The power of the numinous lies beyond the effect it has on the ego nature. The uniqueness of this form of experience is in its capacity to shift an individual's perception and consciousness in an instant. This divine, transcendent experience of the numinous must be honored—it is a way that soul can immediately make its presence known.

My Numinous Experience

Before I discuss my numinous experience, I want to address some of my contextual factors. As a young adult I was not spiritual—in fact, I did not even know what that word really meant. When I think about my early childhood days and the contextual factors surrounding my spirituality, I remember going to the Sunday school affiliated with the Ukrainian Greek Orthodox Church that my family attended. I have fond memories of the priest walking down the isle wearing ornate robes carrying a small smoke pot of holy incense. However, when I was about twelve, my parents purchased a small family business, a dry good store, and everything changed. The entire family had to work to prepare the business for the following week, so church on Sunday became a thing of the past. I had no other spiritual roadmaps, except for an inner voice deep within.

Eventually my parents sold their dry goods store in Two Hills, and moved the family to Edmonton, where they purchased a hotel, our new family business. In my early twenties as I was living in Edmonton and working in the family hotel business after my brother Doug's death, I realized that this was not the direction that I wanted my life to go, so I kept on searching for a way out. I continued to model and decided to take some acting classes, loved them, and eventually went back to university to complete my degree in drama. Acting classes enabled me to go deeper inside of myself and gave me a deeper experience of the fashion show stage that I so enjoyed being on. Acting helped me to build a bridge from the shallow part of myself to the deeper aspects of the human experience through the characters that I played. I was not only able to express inner truths, but go to places emotionally that I had never been before. I met amazing teachers and mentors who challenged my emotional capacities, and I felt myself growing because of it. The process of healing the shallowness that haunted me in my past had begun, and I liked that.

In addition to studying acting, I also studied voice and soon realized what a transformative modality it was for me. During my mid twenties, through the study of voice, I experienced my alienation and disconnection from my body and soul. My voice teacher made me very aware of this disconnection and made me do a series of techniques to break through the barriers. One day in class, I had an unexpected cathartic experience; I began shaking, dropped to the floor in a fetal-like position, and sobbed for what seemed like eternity—it felt as if my insides were exploding. I simultaneously felt shame, shock, and awe, as I experienced a heightened state of sexual energy surge throughout my body. I had no idea what had happened to me, but I knew this was unlike anything that had ever happened to me before. All I could do was to lay there and surrender.

After this experience subsided I intuitively knew that my life had changed, but I couldn't articulate it. Over the next few days I noticed that I no longer treated my body as an object to be dressed and fed, but as a living home for my soul. I noticed that the way that I moved about in the world and related to people was different—my perception was clearer. I had a deeper respect for my body and would listen to that inner voice. I now made a conscious choice to eat healthy organic foods, take long baths filled with aromatherapy and sea salts, as well as get regular massages. Clearly this experience changed my relationship with my body and soul, because I did not do these things prior to the experience. I also noticed different nuances and textures in my voice that felt strangely familiar, and for the first time in my life I could understand the concept of an *authentic voice*. This numinous event brought me an embodied experience of the power of voice and kept me studying voice. My life journey was tremendously influenced by this experience with voice. It was twenty-plus years before I learned what had happened to me—a numinous experience.

This numinous experience guided me to study voice with some extraordinary mentors and voice teachers. My educational pursuits expanded my knowledge and deepened my intellect and understanding of the body-voice-soul connection. My non linear path had so many twists and turns that I don't think anyone could have even predicted the result. Voice is my passion; it is connected to the part of the soul that holds the destiny or potential of a person, a blueprint for its destiny. *The Transformational Power of Voice,* my first book, was inspired by this numinous experience. Clearly, all those years I was on a soul journey, but I had no idea at the time.

Spiritual Experiences

Spiritual experiences, in contrast to numinous experiences, are chosen events that can move us from one level of consciousness to another one. The purpose of spiritual experiences is to connect an individual with divine energy. Clearly there are many ascending levels of possibility, and everyone's journey and desire are very unique. Spiritual experiences come in many forms. Some have formal practices that include prayer, ritual, spiritual practice, and ceremony, as occur in Native American, Hindu, Judeo-Christian, Muslim, and shamanic traditions, to name a few. Some individuals prefer a more informal process, based on ideas from a combination of different traditions that are not conflicting, because each individual has a unique perspective and idea about what is spiritual. The pathways of all spiritual traditions can lead to a happy life as well to divine spiritual experiences. Even though some spiritual experiences may be more structured than others, the connecting quality is that they lay a pathway for soul energy to experience *oneness with the universe.* Structured spiritual examples include pilgrimages to Mecca to deepen one's connection to Allah, Native American sweat lodges to foster inner visions, Hindu mantra practice to increase inner vibrations to connect with divine energies, and Christian prayer using the rosary to deepen devotion to God, just to name a few. Unstructured spiritual experiences may also be poignant and transformative, as is reflected in my personal story.

Jasmine's Spiritual Experience

Jasmine, a beautiful vivacious redhead, came to my office to work through some relationship issues. In the first session she related the following story because she wanted to be sure that I would honor her blend of Hindu and shamanic spirituality and beliefs during our therapy sessions. The story she told me follows:

I was in India meditating in small area near a sacred fountain at the Spiritual Center. My master came by and asked me to meet him later that day for a private teaching. I was thrilled. I went to the appointed place, a small room that smelled of exquisite incense. As I sat on the mat in front of this amazing holy man, he began the session with a prayer, then he took a red rose from the altar, clipped off the stem and put it into his hands. He asked me what was in his hand, and I of course told him it was a red rose. Then he told to me say my *personal mantra,* which no one is supposed to know except me. I recited it silently, like I was taught to do, but all of a sudden I remember being confused about what it was. Nevertheless I kept on saying it anyway. And then I watched him crush the rose in his hands. After a few minutes he asked me again what was in his hand, and I said a crushed red rose. Then he opened his hand again and there was a lingam (a black stone used for healings). The crushed rose was gone. I was shocked—I had watched his hands the entire time. He then gave me the lingam and told me to keep it with me at all times for protection. Later that night I had a dream in which the master came in my dream world and told me my correct personal mantra and went over the correct pronunciation of it, because I had it wrong when I was saying it silently. I woke up in a sweat . . . astonished.

Jasmine's spiritual experience integrates Hindu spiritual ceremony, practice, and devotion. This was an initiation practice bound in tradition and ceremony that had been passed down through the centuries to those who were ready to move through to the next ascending level. Clearly Jasmine had entered that realm. She was able to observe and be present to the limitless possibilities of divine spiritual energy. Her story also incorporates a miraculous sequence as evidenced by the change in form of a crushed rose to a lingam.

Katie's Spiritual Experience

I met Katie, a Christian "deliverance minister," while we were being interviewed as experts in our chosen fields regarding the movie *"The Last Exorcist."* Months after our initial meeting, we began working on another project. One day she told me this story about an exorcism with which she was involved.

> I was working on a case where a client was possessed for nine months. Several exorcisms had taken place since the intake was done and a total of nineteen demons were already expelled. Today another exorcism was planned. As I sat there in preparation of the event, I looked into this client's eyes and every hair on my arms stood up. I expected that a physical attack could come at any moment, but then I covered myself with the armor of God. Now let me tell you, this is not imaginary armor. I can see it, feel its weight, and smell the steal it is made out of. We took the client to the chapel, as usual. The client was wrapped in a sheet and seated in a chair. There were three exorcists and two deacons. The Rite of Exorcism began and the demon fought ferociously in the client's body. When we asked how deliverance would come, after petitioning St. Gabriel for help, the demon finally replied, "On Bloody Mount." We all looked at each other, not quite sure what to think. None of us had heard of this before, and it isn't in the Bible. We then asked by what prayer it would be expelled, and it said, *"The Lord's Prayer."* I thought, what, no difficult prayer that would require deep study to find? So we began, *"Our Father, who Art in Heaven,"* which we said over and over for an hour and a half, all the while asking God, Jesus Christ, the Holy Spirit, the saints, the Blessed Mother, and those who were known to be praying to come stand with us to defeat this demon.

Bloody Mount, Bloody Mount kept going through my head. I looked up from where I was standing and saw it. Bloody Mount was Christ on the crucifix on a small mount. I guess some would call it a hill. But it clicked. With this knowledge we continued with the Lord's Prayer. After nine months of agony and possession, the demon was expelled. Right at this moment a cougar ran past the window for all to see and the client opened his eyes and simultaneously said, "Light."

At the end I could feel that God's presence was there. God himself came to the Deliverance Chapel. Not as the Holy Spirit, but he, himself. Did I see it? No. But did I feel it . . . ? I was brought to my knees, literally brought to my knees in tears. God came in at the same moment that the cougar leaped by. I've said it before but will say it again, with every exorcism I change. I grow closer to God in ways that I never imagined possible. God rocks!

This exorcism was conducted in the Catholic tradition of prayer, ritual, and ceremony. As the demonic force was expelled the divine realms and animal realms acknowledged this extraordinary healing. The cougar symbolized a great mystical transformation of death and rebirth, and the enveloping presence of God symbolized divinity and sanctity of the soul transformation that occurred. When involved with such a powerful healing, the practitioners may simultaneously receive a numinous experience, a divine transformation within their soul, as acknowledged by the inner change that Katie felt. This aspect will be further discussed in the section on the miraculous.

My Spiritual Experience

The entire time that I was studying acting, I kept on modeling, and I remember working with this fabulous Native American designer who inspired me spiritually. Besides admiring his fabulous artistic Indian-inspired creations, I enjoyed speaking with him and discussing his unique spiritual perspectives. I confided in him one night about my unhappiness and desire to live my life differently. He shared with me some incredible Native American myths and stories and suggested I speak to his elder. On my own inkling, I decided to go on a *journey into the woods,* telling no one. I knew the best place for me to do this would be to go back to the area where I was born, Two Hills. Since I knew the back roads, I drove around until I found a forest in which I wanted to spend the night. I was very scared when I found the right spot, I got out the red cloth I had brought, stuffed it with loose tobacco, tied it into a bundle, and then tied the bundle to a tree branch. It was my gift to the nature spirits for allowing me to spend the evening with them. It looked beautiful against the moist, rich, lush, green forest. I waited and finally the darkness arrived. I was very nervous and instead of getting quieter, everything got louder. With each new sound I jumped, and I didn't know how I was going to be able to stay there the entire night, so I began to pray: *Our Father who Art in Heaven . . .* ! I put my experience into words that night:

The Awakening

I was alone
It was a very dark night
I was frightened of the unknown
Nature!
The Controller of life—the Balancer!
Something I had never really experienced before,
I guess we all fear the unknown, the unfamiliar.
Yet, how do I exist? on which plane
Is my world real or superficial?

A friend said: Go experience the true life
Travel Inward—come to terms with yourself,
Realize the gift—the knowledge—the balance of the earth
The harmony of life
The creation from God we exist in, yet ignore.
Dig deep. Dig into your inner soul and discover
Your path in harmony

with all the surrounding forces of nature
Learn and you will reap
The happiness you desire within your soul.

Last night I heard a symphony
No one was playing out of tune
The gentle perfection—
Horns, bass, flute, and strings
All from nature
What have I discovered?
The pleasure in my ears and eyes
No more fear of the unknown.

As I look around at this reality
This gift of perfect harmony from nature,
It was all around before,
But I have only just begun to discover
In Nature
The Balance, The Truth,
The Awakening of Life,
My Own.

I faced my fears that night in those woods. This chosen spiritual experience gave me the ability to make changes and move forward to find my authentic soul-driven life.

In time I completed a bachelor's degree in drama and made a decision to do what my mentor, Dr. Ng, whom I discuss in a later chapter, had suggested so many years prior, to move to Toronto and begin a new life. The *Who am I?* is different from the Who I was at twenty-five. The *Who am I now?* is fully engaged in the heroine's journey—I am a thirty-one-year-old actress with no clear direction except that geographical change and transformation are on my horizon.

In order to have money to establish myself in Toronto, I sold my car for two thousand dollars, the seed money for my future, and shifted my attention toward making a life in a place that I had been to once, eleven years prior, knowing only one person. The night I left Edmonton and moved to Toronto is forever etched in my memory. It was a cold, snowy, evening, January 7th, Ukrainian Christmas Day, which I remember clearly because we had a celebratory dinner with some extended family members. After dinner my family took me to the airport, and as I waved goodbye to them, I cried knowing that I would never come back. I knew that they all expected me to fail, so I turned my head and marched forward with incredible strength and conviction toward a brighter future and a new life. It was the end of another era—I left my family, but this time I didn't physically see them for five years. The move was not easy and I had to face a lot of hard, cold, arduous realities and illusions that I was not emotionally, psychologically, or physically prepared for, but I was always guided to the appropriate healers and mentors, and for that I feel very blessed.

Miraculous Experiences

Miraculous experiences are divine experiences that break the templates of illusion of what we are programmed to see. Miraculous experiences embody miracle energy, and by this I mean that there is a change in any of the elements: air, earth, water, fire, ether, metal, or the condition of life. Miraculous energies take you out of the tunnel vision of your contextual factors and in a moment can change your reality—they are instantaneous experiences beyond the life and death cycle. They pull you out of any reality that you have ever known because they take you beyond three-dimensional reality. Miraculous experiences are similar to numinous experiences, the difference being that numinous experiences occur unexpectedly and are not attached to any spiritual traditions or practices. Miraculous experiences, on the other hand are usually attached to some form of spiritual discipline such as those of Hinduism, Kabala, alchemy, and shamanism, to name a few. It is also important to understand that some spiritual practices can lead to miraculous experiences, and some practitioners may use spiritual practices to perform miracles, wherein they change the dynamics of the elements, or condition of life, as in Jasmine's spiritual experience where she sees the crushed rose change into the lingam. Since miracle energy is beyond our ordinary reality, it makes us question what is true and not true, thereby deconstructing our illusions about life and changing our perception of reality. The bible provides us with examples: Moses sees a burning bush that is unconsumed by fire; Jesus multiplies one fish and one loaf into countless of each to feed the throngs gathered for his teachings; and, Lazarus rises from the dead. These are miraculous energies because there is a change in the quality of the element.

There are two levels of miraculous experiences. The first level happens outside of us, we observe a miracle. An example of this is being told by the doctor that your son would never walk again, and he walks again, or seeing a friend go from HIV+ to HIV-, a medical impossibility. These types of miracles move beyond the boundary of medical science into what is possible but unknown. The underlying factor is that there is a complete change in the condition of the individual or situation. I will address my personal acquaintance with this type of miraculous experience when I discuss my mentor, Dr. Ng, in Chapter Six.

The second type of miraculous experience is more complex and higher on the spectrum of divine experience. These experiences are usually twofold because they include a practitioner and his or her capacity to change an element in some manner. In general, the protocol for an enlightened practitioner from the Hindu tradition, when he or she performs a miracle, is to bring a spark of enlightenment to all who view it, as in Jasmine's example. In this tradition the practitioner is specifically practicing his unordinary ability to break the life and death barrier, which in turn dissolves illusions about life and death that exist within his or her students.

Most practitioners who can enliven the inanimate elements or change the life condition can also enliven themselves in the process. The enlivening of the practitioner would be referred to as numinous, as experienced by Katie as she acknowledges a change, an enlivening in her own nature from her work with the Christian exorcism. In the Hindu tradition, when an enlightened master reintegrates a dead bird back into life it would be called a miraculous event, and the enlivening he experiences though that is not his purpose or intent, would be called numinous. The key to understanding miraculous energy is that something in the elements or life condition needs to be transformed.

Clearly there are areas where the boundaries and definitions of the miraculous, spiritual, and numinous energies intersect, however all three are in the dimension of the divine, with ascending complexity. The difference between a numinous and a miraculous or spiritual experience is that one happens unexpectedly without intention, and the others are based on a spiritual tradition. All three, however, are manifestations of divine energy. On the spectrum of soul engagement, when a practitioner can perform a miracle, and enliven him or herself in this two-fold process would be of the highest complexity and would be considered a combination of both numinous and miraculous energies or numinous and spiritual energies, depending on the situation.

Illiana's Miraculous Experience

Illiana is a therapist and friend of mine. We do not talk often because we both have busy schedules, and she has been spending long periods of time in India working with her spiritual master. However, when we do connect, it is always as if no time has passed between us. When I finally heard from her after several months, she told me that she had been cured of breast cancer. I was thrilled for her but also surprised that I did not even know she had been ill. When I asked her, she said that it had happened so fast that there was no time to tell anyone. Then she told me her miraculous story of the last two months.

> When I came back from India this last time, I had this very powerful dream. In this dream my master's voice told me that I had to have a mammogram immediately because there was a lump in my breast. The message was so strong that I immediately woke up from the dream and checked my breasts. I could feel something and knew I had to get it checked out immediately. Western medicine is not what I normally do, but the power of the dream was so strong that I followed it. The

mammogram did in fact find several lumps in my breast that did not look good. I was, of course, devastated. I calmed myself down by realizing that my spiritual master had told me about this and was already taking care of me. I immediately started taking the blessed waters and powders that I had collected over the years of going to India. By the time I went in for my follow-up breast imaging to prepare me for biopsy, and the new tests showed that the lumps were completely gone. The doctors were shocked. Their response to me was that it was a fibrocystic growth that just dissolved. Then the doctors told me that whatever was there was now completely gone.

My faith was strengthened by this experience of healing. I had heard of others receiving miraculous healings, but to have this happen to me so quickly and clearly changed my faith and my belief that real healing is a miraculous event no matter how it happens.

This experience deepened Illiana's belief and faith in the miraculous powers that exist beyond modern science. She experienced a total realignment and redirection in her life because of this experience. She now has a deeper understanding of the miraculous and a renewed commitment to the powers of healing that exist beyond the normal framework . . . the miraculous.

Crystal's Miraculous Experience

Crystal, a delightful, adventurous, and high-spirited woman, related this story during one of her therapy sessions. She had a history of hormonal imbalances and was told that she would never be able to conceive.

I got pregnant just one time. At the moment of conception I knew that something miraculous had happened. I felt as though the whole world shifted sideways, and

I was somehow beyond my body and in it at the same time. However, the baby died within the first eight weeks. I had to have a D and C to remove the remaining tissue. It was very traumatic for me. I kept crying for months. I could barely understand why this was so traumatic for me, and I didn't know why couldn't I get over this. I never planned to have children because I knew of my hormonal imbalances—so why this upset me so much, I did not know.

The crying was going on far too long, and I felt terrible, so I decided to see a shaman about this issue. In my session with him he looked at me and said that I needed a soul retrieval. He shook a rattle and put me into a trance, and he also went into a trance. He journeyed into the underworld while I lay there in a kind of blank bliss. This went on for what only seemed a few minutes, and then he told me to sit up. He reported that after he had been to my underworld. He saw me there with an old lady next to me. The old lady was very angry and said that I had let something precious be taken from me during the D and C. She handed him a ring, and he placed it back in my belly in the vision.

As we were talking, I felt that this ring was my feminine power. Somehow it had either been scraped out or I had given it away during the D and C, and later through grief. From that day forward I did not cry about the miscarriage again. I had no feelings of remorse or pain. Instead I had a glowing feeling that my pregnancy had given me a divine gift of knowing that essential feminine experience of conception (divine creation) in my own body, and I felt extremely grateful.

The shamanic healing vision embraced the miraculous through tradition and ceremony. Crystal's life condition was altered through the healing. Indeed she was healed beyond the boundary of medical science into what is possible but unknown.

Divine Occurrences

Whether you have a numinous, miraculous, or spiritual or experiences, know that there is a supporting structure, an inner architecture that exists within you. I imagine the inner architecture of soul to be covered by one's sense of self—the polarity of fears and joys—and that layer covered by the contextual factors of lineage. In order for the soul to become known, it must penetrate through those layers. Perhaps this initiation process is necessary for becoming a soul-centered human being. In numinous experiences, for example, intense energy builds in the soul, causing it to push forward through those layers, as in Raina's, Rebecca's, Chalice's, and my cathartic experiences. In miraculous or spiritual experiences, the mechanism that penetrates through the layers is built into the particular tradition. I imagine the mechanism to be like a drill making a hole through the layers so that the soul can emerge as we can see from the stories of Jasmine, Illiana, Katie, and Crystal. The "drill" is some form of prayer, spiritual practice, ceremony or ritual, depending on your religious background. You must also be open to the divine energy of unconditional love and you must suspend judgment and release doubts so that the soul experience can take you to where it needs to go, rather than your taking control over it. Soul transformation is the result of being open to the gifts of the cosmos. If you try to control the spiritual process you will abort it. Instead, surrender and go with the divine flow of life.

Engaging your soul, whether through a numinous, spiritual, or miraculous, experiences embodies cosmic divinity. Even though there are many forms, traditions, styles, combinations, and ways to engage divine energy an unknown factor is always present because these experiences may occur unexpectedly as in the numinous experience. However, you can make a choice to develop you own experience of divinity and engage in your own spiritual process, as I did. If you don't have a process that inspires you, explore different spiritual traditions, especially those that are different from those that you are familiar to give you a more expansive overview. Only then can you make a well-informed choice. Or you can even decide on integrating a combination of spiritual traditions as long as they support your process. Clearly everyone is unique and there is no one-size-fits-all formula when you embark on a spiritual path. Engaging your soul, the Invisible Actor within is an amazing process. It is also a time when you should pay more attention to your dreams and inner voices, because they will also guide you toward soul transformation.

There are also many other ways to engage with soul that are less intense and that can be done on a daily basis. Some of these include meditation, spending time in nature, listening to music, doing some form of voicework, viewing incredible art, practicing yoga, listening to tapes from spiritual teachers, engaging in breathwork, hugging and holding your pets, analyzing your dreams, paying attention to synchronistic experiences, doing charity work, praying, and living your life with integrity. These are just a few ways that you can choose to connect to the Invisible Actor within.

Exploring Your Soul Engagement

Exploring your story of soul engagement and journaling about it is a very satisfying experience. Concretizing your story enlivens the Invisible Actor within. If you have not had this type of experience, you can always create one by taking an active role. First I would suggest that you write about your options, then do it! *Your life is your creation!*

PART II
HOW TO
DECONSTRUCT
YOUR
ILLUSIONS

CHAPTER 5

THE ILLUSIONS WE HOLD SO DEAR

On September 11, 2001, the illusion that the United States was impenetrable by terrorists literally crashed into reality with the collapse of the Twin Towers, the destruction of part of the Pentagon, and the plane crash near Shanksville in rural Pennsylvania. Nearly three thousand victims and nineteen hijackers died in the attacks. On April 19, 1995, in Oklahoma City, the illusion that terrorists come from other countries crashed into reality with the bombing of the Federal Building by Timothy McVeigh, a fellow American. One hundred and sixty-eight victims died in the attack. On December 7, 1941, the illusion that the Japanese would never attack America crashed into reality with the attack on Pearl Harbor. Over two thousand victims died in the attack. Each one of these attacks profoundly shocked the American people and forever changed their reality. The illusion of who and what Americans thought they were became a different reality after each of these events.

Thinkers from far-flung fields—spiritual traditions, philosophers, artists, and scientists, have suggested that everything we take to be true or real in the world is actually an illusion. Albert

Einstein declared "Reality is merely an illusion, albeit a persist-ent one." T.S. Elliot professed that "Humankind cannot bear very much reality." Sigmund Freud revealed "Illusions commend themselves to us because they save us pain and allow us to enjoy pleasure instead. We must therefore accept them without com-plaint when they sometimes collide with a bit of reality against which they are dashed to pieces." Each of these statements open up the complexity of these two words: *illusion* and *reality*.

Illusion and Reality

I examine the concepts of illusion and reality through a psycho-logical lens to help you become more aware of the world in which you are actually living. Illusions and realities are intricate and complex because they are ephemeral and shift according to our life situation and consciousness level. I define illusions as imaginal beliefs that are co-created by our self and our contextual factors. Illusions feel like, look like, or are imagined to be something that they are not; they are interpretations of a situation that become our version of the story, but they may not be the reality of the situation. For example, if we show five people a video of a cou-ple fighting at the kitchen table in front of their ten-year-old son, we will most likely get five different perspectives of the situation. Person One is currently involved in a custody battle and is so focused on the inappropriateness of the parents fighting at the dinner table. Person Two, with a history of childhood abuse, is horrified by the parents abuse of their young son. Person Three has critical mother issues and is disgusted with the husband's criticalness of his wife. Person Four has done some assertiveness training courses and is glad that the wife is standing up to her husband and Person Five, a conflict resolution counselor, feels that fighting is necessary at times because it allows for a change in the dynamics of a relationship. Each person's perception of the situation is different because of his or her contextual factors, which in turn shapes the individual's personal values, morals, and priorities of perceptions and understandings of how life works.

Perception can be thought of as an individual's interpretation of the interplay of past experiences and contextual factors. *Is your glass half full or half empty?* is a great example. Perception is one of the oldest fields of psychology. Psychologists use tests like those of the Rorschach and the Thematic Apperception Test (TAT) to assess an individual's personality structure using inkblots or pictures to engage a person's internal perceptual experience. According to the assumptions on which these texts are based the manner in which we process the data of a situation or event is arranged by perceptual sets in the brain that are formed from our life experiences or perhaps have even been handed down through the family line. What you must become acutely aware of is that you are born into a world that has already been organized prior to your birth and as you enter this reality, you believe this reality, because it is all you know—the impersonal contextual factors. You do not know another reality so you believe your reality to be true, and your brain confirms that conclusion. This is why it is hard to comprehend other realities. Unfortunately, we do not come into the world with mental flexibility; it is something that must be learned and learning it as an adult is not an easy process.

Illusions occur on multiple levels and are related to the psychological depth and acumen of an individual. Illusions engage our perceptual viewpoint, like a big movie screen in a theatre, which is why they are so hard to see. They are our inner world perceptions appearing in projected form, taking center stage. We are also in an illusion about our environment unless something or someone pulls us out. Since we can't recognize an illusion ourselves, we need a life-altering experience. Such an experience can come from either end of the spectrum, good or bad. Disasters, traumas, crisis, or curve balls are at one end of the spectrum, whereas mentors, spiritual teaches, psychologists, or even a good self-help book are at the other end, all assisting you to awaken to your reality. These experiences are trying to assist us in one-way or another to shift our perceptions. When these life-altering situations occur, our inner world collapses or realigns, which in turn pushes us into another psychological state: chaos. When we break an illusion, we find something inside of ourselves that is eternal and truthful and that brings forth a new level of consciousness, and provides us with an opportunity to recognize these illusions. Unfortunately the only way to know we are in an illusion is in retrospect. We are all really in a fish bowl of our own design and setup but we don't know it. When we see the reality of an illusion, then that illusion is gone and a new one forms—it's the process of life until we reach stage five, continual soul engagement.

There is always an intense resistance to the breaking of an illusion because the illusion is created by our interpretations and perceptions of our past experiences and contextual factors. The problem is that every interpretation of a situation becomes proof of the contextual factors into which we were born or serve to validate its principles, which in turn further strengthens the illusions in which we live. Bottom line: our stories validate our illusions, which in turn reinforce our contextual illusions—a vicious cycle of unconscious processes.

Resistance to breaking an illusion causes suffering. For example, if a husband walks out on his wife, she suffers and then creates a sad story about what happened to her. With this sad story her suffering increases and her story, in turn gets bigger. Suffering always gets more intense if we resist breaking an illusion. The resistance to breaking an illusion is worse than the actuality of breaking the illusion. The breaking of an illusion feels like a terrible loss, a loss of an old way of being, a deconstruction of our reality, a death experience. In this case if the wife gave up her illusion that marriage is forever, instead of getting entrenched in "this shouldn't happen to me" victim mindset, she could move toward a place of healing. This example of suffering and the choices we make illuminates the life-and-death cycle at play.

The impetus for breaking an illusion comes from the Invisible Actor. Life, it presents us with a situation in which we have an opportunity to learn a lesson. If we don't learn the lesson, we will be presented with another similar lesson each time the lesson's impact will increase in intensity until we do get the point that our soul wants us to get.

Jack came in and told me how much he hated his job and that two years ago, he'd fallen down the stairs at work and really hurt himself. He got treated, but six months later part of the ceiling in his office collapsed on top of him. He was treated again, and then he got a new supervisor that was so abusive that he did not know what to do—which is why he ended up in my office. I told Jack that he should look for another job, and his only response was to offer five or six excuses about why he shouldn't leave his job, that all of his problems were one hundred percent the fault of his new boss. He wasn't even able to consider that perhaps the universe, or his Invisible Actor, wanted something different for him. He was so stuck in his fear-based contextual factors that he was paralyzed. You also see this process everyday in life, just look at your friends and co-workers. My advice is: *Always work to break the illusions, go through the pain of change, and move forward in your life.*

When you are off-balance, your illusions will appear very clearly and you will hit reality. While writing this chapter, I was off balance because I was working overly hard, to the exclusion of everything else, and found myself caught in being a *doing machine*, an old pattern of mine (which I will discuss in Chapter Eleven) and just kept on pushing until my illusions came into focus. It was a very painful process in the short term but immensely relieving in the long term. Illusion breaking can come from the inside or from the outside of you—no one is exempt and no one can be protected from the process. However, you must be very careful, because there are many ways to reinterpret and preserve an illusion. Your shadow side, a concept I will explore in a later chapter, can circumvent an illusion if you are not careful. For example, if you are a me-centered individual, you may retreat back to the egotistical state of the narcissist—*it's all about me*—which further locks you into the illusion. This is a common fall-back position, especially for men, so be awake. When you retreat to your fall-back position you are in the darker and more shadowy part of your personality, and you don't even know it. Many people get stuck there and play the same unhealthy pattern over and over, the only difference being is that the intensity of the situations will increase until they get the message.

Reality, on the other hand, can be thought of as what actually exists in our world—the absence of illusion. It is the *what is* of a situation. Reality, in its truest form, is devoid of our perceptions, beliefs, or contextual factors. The truest forms of reality do not exist psychologically because we have a reality that is always layered with perspectives and perceptions from our lineage, our contextual factors, and the physical body itself. Psychologically speaking, *the trouble with reality is that it is always changing*. Our reality changes because of life-altering experiences, shifts in consciousness, soul stirrings and soul engagements, as well as physiologically through the aging process along the lifespan. When we finally get comfortable with ourselves and the reality of our lives, we have a birthday, hit another decade, and with that comes a new level of consciousness as well as a new set of issues with which we have to deal.

We have all heard the *What is a chair?* riddle. In a certain form, a shape is perceived to be a chair, but if we cut that shape into two, three, four, or six pieces, is it still a chair? It could be referred to as *pieces of a chair*, but there is no actual chair left. So, is the chair an illusion or a reality? Or has the reality of the chair shifted? It is clear that the chair in its form no longer exists. So what is the reality of chair? Perhaps the essence of reality is that *"It's nothing but a collective lunch!"* as penned by author Jane Wagner. The intricate interweaving of concepts such as illusion and reality is much easier to be seen through a chair story than in our own lives.

Chalice's Story

An exquisite, African American woman, Chalice (whose numinous experience I recounted in Chapter Four), thirty-one, came into my office for a consultation. I noticed how beautifully dressed she was as she gracefully glided into the treatment room and arranged herself on my couch. She worked as a speech therapist and had just broken up with her boyfriend, a man she believed that she'd marry. She told me that she had read *The Transformational Power of Voice*, my first book, and felt that she was acting like Echo, in the myth of Echo and Narcissus, and did not want to partake in that type of behavior any more. The heartbreak of losing her potential husband collapsed her inner structures and we both knew that change was in the horizon—that is, if she wanted to go there. She had a passion for ballet and used ballet classes to help her physically work through her heartbreak. She proceeded to tell me her story of illusion and reality, just as I was struggling with writing this chapter. Was this synchronicity, angels, or the Invisible Actor guiding me?

Chalice told me that last week after receiving an abusive text from her former boyfriend, she was very upset and decided to go to a ballet class to relieve some tension. As she was doing her bar routine, she noticed that she was observing herself through her boyfriend's eyes, imagining that he was watching her move through her ballet routine with great delight. She was actually admiring herself through the eyes of the *other* in order to feel good about herself—the Echo myth. This realization shocked her. She had taken on her boyfriend's identity as a way to feel his imagined adoration as he watched her perform. She found this was very disturbing. Her analytic mind realized what she was doing and she tried to redirect her energies toward herself and her body, but it was very hard for her to be present with herself without creating someone else imaginally to observe her. Then came another devastating moment when she realized that she does this all the time—Chalice always sees herself through the lens of the *other* and not through her own eyes.

Chalice became acutely conscious of the illusion in which she was caught—the disempowered feminine on multiple levels. Her past was full of negative experiences with males, she was sexually molested as a child by her uncle, her father abandoned her when she was four and died of a drug overdose when she was fifteen, she had a string of handsome narcissistic boyfriends who never valued her, and she was having a hard time finding Mr. Right. So how could Chalice find her life partner when she was caught in the illusions that were created because of her perceptions and contextual factors. Her illusions include: I need to have the adoration of a man in order to feel good about myself, I can only feel good about myself through the eyes of another, and I can't validate myself. Illusions do not emerge from the void but from our own life experiences and the interpretations of our story and contextual factors. She defined herself through *other,* like Echo, and perhaps that was why she never made it as a professional dancer—she was not dancing to her own "music."

In the myth Echo loses her voice and body as a result of her illusions. In the first part of the Echo myth she is cursed by the goddess Hera for deceiving the feminine powers, the goddess looking for wholeness from the gods, the masculine. Hera curses her by taking away her creative ability to speak, so Echo can now only repeat, or copy, what she hears. In the second phase of the story, Echo loses her body as a result of her illusions of loving Narcissus, an extraordinarily beautiful man. What Echo falls in love with is her *projected* image of Narcissus, a man who is incapable of ever engaging in a relationship—it is impossible love.

Chalice's perceptions imposed upon her the illusion that if a man adores you, then you are valued and validated. Millions of people all over the world that do this—it is an archetypal pattern. The illusion of form, or *other*, as a manifestation of love, is an illusion. There is absolutely no possibility of true love when you are engaged in this unhealthy pattern. It doesn't matter if you are a man or a woman, straight or gay.

Clearly there are a lot of other illusions and unhealthy projections and patterns that Chalice had to work on, but she was ready to move forward and connect with the healthier side of her personality by taking back her feminine nature and her body. Breaking an illusion is an intense experience, because it is the reality of the situation that makes you feel like you were living a lie. Beneath that illusion we connect to our eternal essence, our soul. Even though becoming conscious of illusions is shockingly painful, the inspiration of what is real ultimately brings transformation.

Chalice worked very hard in therapy to reconnect with her feminine creative nature, to value herself, and to not look for another man to validate her so that she could feel that she was okay. When she can own and self-validate her own feminine power she will attract a totally different type of man. Our inner world creates our outer world—*always*!!!

The Echo myth is an archetypal story of creation. All human beings create their illusions based on *other*—there is no other way. Our sense of self, like Echo, is based on *other* because we cannot develop in a void. If the Echo myth illuminates the nature of illusion creation, then every creation of reality is a representation of Echo. Echo is entranced by an illusion that takes her to her death and disembodiment, a pathological state. Perhaps this is a possibility of what will happen to us if we don't face our illusions. Let's face it: we are all in love with our own reflection, and if everything in life is a reflection, then we are making love with our own Echo. The problem occurs when we are in the shadowy side of our personality because the illusion could become pathological, as Echo demonstrates. Without understanding this illusion creation process, as enacted in the myth of Narcissus and Echo, we cannot come to know our own soul, the eternal flame within.

Breaking our illusions is a difficult and painful experience because doing so takes the floor out from under us, so to speak and catapults us on the path of change. We do not usually go out of our way to unmask from our illusions because it is painful—usually we go kicking and screaming all the way. However, change is always on the horizon for all of us, whether we want it or not. Illusions affect our perceptions of reality, and broken illusions are part of the reality of life. We must understand both aspects, and we must always recognize that we have a limited perception of reality because of our contextual factors. We can be smart, educated, and yet totally blinded by our illusions, as clearly evidenced in Chalice's case. The sad reality is that everyone on the planet fits into this category, and it is hard for any of us to see our own illusions, including me. Perhaps reality is our own hand-painted canvas, co-created with a template that has been handed down through the generations that contains the images and symbols of our chaotic world—the past, present, and future—a creative illusion that we use as a standard by which to live. We imaginally hang this painting in the recesses of our mind and attach to it, to remind us who we are or who we think we are. Who wants to change their painting by choice? It defines us. But does it?

Breaking our painted realities, our illusions, can be achieved through serious psychological work, encounters with others, and soul transformation approaches. You may begin your own process with mentors, spiritual teachers, psychologist, or self-help books so that you can move forward towards the process of change. However, when illusion breaking comes from the numinous, spiritual, or miraculous, it allows for a more direct and streamlined approach because these processes enable you to go beyond your boundaries and connect directly to your Invisible Actor. When this happens, your soul is engaged, enlivened, and primed to take you to new areas of reality, authenticity, and truthful adventure... the hero and heroine's journey.

Grace's Story

You have all heard the saying, *wake up to your life*. Waking up to life means facing your illusions and dealing with the reality of your situation. Most people come into therapy because their reality and their ideal situation are on opposite sides of the universe. One day a fashionably dressed woman named Grace sauntered into my office and stated that she was living her life spiritually and was waiting for her soul mate to show up, but so far he hadn't made his appearance. In reality, she had not dated or been in a relationship for twelve years, she was now forty-five, and she probably was not ever going to have a baby— all of which was devastating to her. She felt that just by doing her spiritual practice and living her life with integrity that the right man would just show up, though she was not putting herself *"out there"* in the world to meet anyone. Unfortunately, the days of the white knights galloping on white horses and rescuing young maidens are gone, but they still live in our myths and in our minds. There comes a time when every women has to deal with this white-knight issue. Clearly Grace was caught up in multiple illusions but I will only address two of them. She placed herself in the role of the victim, on two levels: if I am good and pretty then a man will rescue me; and, if I perform spiritual practices, then the universe will bring a man to me. The sad part of her story is that she lost twelve years in distorted illusions with the center of power lying outside her. In the process Grace became very me-centered and didn't even realize it.

Getting psychological counseling to help her see her destructive patterns was absolutely necessary to achieve her hearts desire for love, compassion, and romance.

When you work with your illusions, you take responsibility for your life so that you can wake up from a dream state. Becoming conscious of your old reality and moving forward to a new reality, a new version of your self, is the process of change—*becoming the new version of you*. I believe that our self-painting, our artistic creation, is a work in progress, with the colors, symbols, and hues, changing and deepening as we move through the life cycle, yet at each point, this painting holds the essence of the authentic self that is exploring the many ascending spheres of growth. Life involves constant change, forward movement; reality shifts. It is a relentless process of waking up to new creations of reality that is, if you choose to wake up so that you can be present and conscious in your life. Your life painting is complete only when you leave this physical plane; it is the archetypal imprint of your life story—your personal mythology of your time on earth.

Fred and Freida's Story

Life is full of events, situations, illusions, perceptions, projections, and interpretations. Some we choose to partake in willingly, and some we don't. Sex is an event that most everyone wants to engage in, whatever your sexual orientation. We all want it, fantasize about it, and look for it using various options. It is a multi-trillion dollar business. Talking about sex and people's realities and illusions about sex in the therapy room is always interesting. A couple, Fred and Freida, came into therapy to work on their troubled two-year marriage. Now we all know the old adage: *Nothing screws up a marriage faster than sex and money, not enough or too much in either direction*. Just open any tabloid and read about the latest sexual shenanigans of the rich-and-famous sports stars, politicians, and celebrities. It's a socially accepted form of voyeurism.

In the initial stages of therapy, I like to discuss a couple's sex life because it gives me an indication as to the level of emotional deterioration or health of their relationship. So when I asked Fred and Freida if they were still having sex, they both nodded their head in an up-and-down movement, and I took this as a positive sign. However, when I asked Fred if his sex life was satisfying, he angrily stated that he hardly ever had sex and that he was not getting his sexual needs met in the relationship. Freida became visibly upset at his response and defended herself saying that they had sex all the time, in fact, far too much sex. When I finally got them to calm down, they both agreed that they had sex on the average of three to four times per week. At that point I was thrilled to get a consensus. Statistics show that healthy couples, on the average, have sex one to three times a week. Fred felt that he was starving sexually and Freida felt that she was saturated and overwhelmed sexually. The reality of the event, and its frequency, were agreed upon, but their perceptions of their experiences were on different ends of the polarities. They both said that they loved each other and they wanted to make their marriage work. As a psychologist I can tell you: *Love is not enough—it's only step one.* The work in the therapy room is never easy, and sometimes it is hard to find middle ground. In their case I needed a shot of miraculous energy, but didn't know how to channel any. Fred and Freida came to therapy only three times and it is not surprising that their marriage ended. They couldn't agree on most relational issues. Their problems were much deeper than sex—their illusions, projections, and perceptions of marriage were askew. The question I asked myself is: How and why did these two people ever get together and get married?

Illusions and realities are poignant concepts that we have to deal with. They are projected everywhere all the time on multiple levels and in multiple ways, whether you realize it or not. Breaking our illusions can provide us with tremendous healing reactions. They open up new dimensions in our life, further expanding our consciousness level, connecting us to the eternal essence that lives within, the Invisible Actor, the guide of our destiny. I like what the enlightened Hindu Master Sri Kaleshwar Swami teaches: Knowing your reality is your duty and life path.

CHAPTER 6

DECONSTRUCTING ILLUSIONS

econstructing illusions is the fourth stage of soul transformation. This phase begins in early adulthood and continues throughout the lifespan. Illusions, as previously noted are imaginal beliefs that are co-created by us and our contextual factors. They are what we want to believe about a situation, but they are not the reality of the situation. They are the unconscious beliefs, patterns, and projections that have been etched into our psyche from birth and onward. We are completely unaware of their presence because they have become the way that we function in the world and are what I refer to as our *software operating systems*. A perfect analogy of this unconscious process is a fish swimming in water—the fish doesn't know that it is wet. You can't tell the fish that it is wet, nor can you educate it about wetness. The only thing you can do is to take the fish out of its environment. When you do that, you will see the fish squirm and jump and try to get back into the water. Its limited consciousness grasps that it is out of its water element and that it needs to get back to its wetness to survive. Yet there is another unthinkable reality that its limited consciousness does not comprehend—that you will be eating it for lunch.

Deconstructing illusions is the psychological aspect of soul transformation, a process of peeling away the layers of illusions—what we thought our reality was versus what it actually is—a very painful process of self-discovery. When we see our reality clearly for the first time, it shocks us and pushes us toward consciousness and transformation. During these times we ask ourselves questions such as *How did this happen?* and *How did I get here?* The great thing about recognizing these illusions is that they move us toward change.

Some individuals delight in the discovery of their illusions, whereas others stay caught in them, locked and paralyzed with fear, spinning their tires going nowhere. Illusions come in many forms and are layered because they are related to the contextual factors that are etched in your psyche. Here are seven examples of illusions:

1. "My parents promised they would always take care of me—but instead they got drunk and abandoned me."

2. "I was always told that if I followed my bliss, the money would come—but that hasn't happened."

3. "I did what my parents told me: I became a doctor which they said would give me a happy life—but instead I am miserable."

4. "My parents said that they would always be there to support me—but they didn't."

5. "My parents told me that they were working hard for my future and that I must help them accomplish their goals—but in the end my parents squandered their fortune, leaving me and my siblings with nothing but debt."

6. "I believed that if I was a good person, good things would happen to me—but they don't."

7. "I believed that if I was a great employee, my boss would take care of me—but instead he laid me off after twenty

years of outstanding service and replaced me with a twenty-four-year-old."

Contextual factors are poignant and come in many forms as you can see from the above examples. I knew someone who was in an unhappy long-term marriage and very soon after his wife's death from anal cancer, which she had been fighting for ten years, he found love. He confided to me that he felt happy and alive for the first time in many years, yet, as I watched his process, I noticed that he was not willing to give up his old life and habits (his contextual factors) to accommodate his new life and future wife. For example, he was not willing to change his longstanding Friday night manicure appointments, or change his Saturday morning breakfast with the boys, or adjust the time frame for his Sunday morning hikes with his son and grandson, or even include his new love in any of these activities. Fear of change was his driving force. I watched him end a great relationship and return to a life filled with patterns that were based on an unhappy past. He was unwilling to change or adjust patterns that were created as a reaction to an unhappy situation and create healthy patterns for a new life. Instead he became consumed with keeping everything status quo, even though his reality had changed. He was so caught in unhealthy patterns that he actually believed he was moving forward by desperately clinging to the patterns of his past. His fear of change de-energized the Invisible Actor, leaving it lying limp and neglected within.

Now, think of your life and how you respond to situations of change. Ask yourself the following five questions:

1. Do you like change?

2. Do you have a difficult time with change?

3. How do you move toward new areas of possibility?

4. How do you create change in your life?

5. How do you jump out of the box that has confined and defined you?

If you don't like change and resist it at every turn, there are three common stances you need to be aware of. The first one is that you are caught in your contextual factors, and that is a good awareness to have because those factors can have a stronghold over the choices you make. Second, if you don't like change, you may be *caught in a web of fear.* Fear impels you to keep your old patterns alive—you fight for control over what you know. As bizarre as this sounds, just look around at your friends and family members who do not want to change. *Fear is being afraid to wake up to the illusions that engulf you, whereas change involves deconstructing the illusions that surround you.* Third, if you don't like change, you may be moving toward the darker aspects of your personality and perhaps engaging in negative roles such as that of the victim or narcissist. This area will be addressed further in the next chapter.

Some people may have one pivotal event or person that catalyzes change in them while others experience a series of events or have a series of individuals that helps them move forward. Each individual's journey of deconstructing of illusions is unique. Facing your fears moves you toward deconstructing your illusions and acknowledging the pendulum of thoughts and emotions, the positive and negative thoughts and feelings that open up the possibility of choice on many levels. When it comes to change we always have a choice. We may not like the choice that we have, but we always have one. *If you don't like the situation that you are in, and you can't change it, the only thing that you can do is to change your relationship to the situation.* Focusing on life from a perspective of choice and personal responsibility can have a tremendously positive effect on your life because you are changing the illusions that shape your daily experience.

I remember a time early in my career when I was working in a clinical position with a very narcissistic boss. He was demanding, demeaning, and continually pushed me to see more patients. Needless to say I began to hate my job, felt exhausted, and dreaded waking up every morning to go to work. So, I decided to do two things: look for another job and change my relationship to my job. Rather than seeing my job as a human factory, I decided to look at it as a laboratory for the study of human nature. I found this new attitude to be inspiring. I also decided to recreate my relationship with my boss by focusing on his positive qualities. In time my boss stopped badgering me and began to respect my boundaries—which came as a surprise to me. He began to listen to me in ways that he was unable to prior and subsequently reduced my client load to one that was more appropriate. As a result my attitude toward my job changed and I began to feel happy. I did go on a couple of job interviews, but they were not the right fit. By changing the relationship to my situation, my job was changing and I was once again inspired to do the work that I was doing.

Life is about change as represented in the eternal cycle of life and death—a continuous movement from being *in form and out of form*—a constant life pattern. Thus *to fear change is to fear the very essence of life.* The Invisible Actor can be thought of as an eternal change mechanism. Fear disempowers the Invisible Actor within by disabling growth and killing the possibility for change. If you are not allowing the eternal life-death cycle to occur in your life by gradually ending your illusions, you are not living your authentic soul-driven life. And you need to ask yourself: *Is this really how I want to live—shackled to illusions?*

The Deconstruction Phase

Deconstructing your illusions is all about change, and change is the essence and pulse of life. If you don't like change, you need a whole new set of mantras:

1. Change is enlightening.
2. Change is transformational.
3. Change is thrilling.
4. Change is adventurous.
5. Change is invigorating.

Pick one or create your own and move forward! Change is an integral part of life, but no one tells you that. I wonder why? If you are not happy, *change,* because your happiness is absolutely in your control. We all choose everything in our lives, either consciously or unconsciously, so we must face ourselves fully, because hiding only exacerbates the problem we are trying so hard to ignore.

When you begin to deconstruct your illusions, there are two initial steps you must follow:

1. Accept the fact that you have created your situation as the creator of your life.

2. Take back your power and be responsible for your life and what has happened to you.

For example, if you had a bad marriage, you must take responsibility for that relationship because you married the guy or gal. He may have been a jerk, but you did say *I do* in front of the officiator of the marriage ceremony. A shotgun wedding that was arranged by your family and that you were forced into would demonstrate the intense levels of constriction in your family. Nevertheless, you had a part in it, so own it, stay away from the victim role, and move forward! If you do not own your role in the wounding situation or experience, you cannot own the solution either, because you are not in control of solving the problem. If you do not take responsibility for the causality of your life, then you cannot change it.

Deconstructing your illusions is a painful but also exhilarating process of separating from the contextual factors of the conscious and unconscious projections and illusions of your family, friends, culture, community, career, religion, geographic location, environment, political milieu, and government as well as your intense personal experiences. Your gift for doing this will be an increase in personal consciousness and a sharper awareness of who you are authentically.

The Mirror Exercise

Deconstruction targets come into focus when you are unhappy about the manner in which your life is going. You may not really understand why you are unhappy, but your discomfort has ignited an inner dialogue in order to begin to answer the question of *Who am I?* The mirror is always a good place to start. Michael Jackson wrote an amazing song entitled *Man in the Mirror* that dealt with change from an internal perspective. Michael Jackson knew that change is a personal choice and that it can only come from within one's own soul. Gandhi said something similar a half century earlier: "Be the change you want to see in the world." So stand in front of a mirror, take off your clothes, and really look at yourself. Own who you are at that moment, and don't get caught in the judgmental traps of "I need to lose 10 pounds," or "I need to go to the gym," or "I need to get liposuction." *I am who I am! An original human being in a life process that is ever changing and ever growing, and I am exactly where I need to be at this moment.* As you stand in front of the mirror, ask yourself these eight questions:

1. Do I like myself?

2. Am I a happy person?

3. Am I happy about the way that my life is going?

4. Am I an honest and truthful person? Or does that need work?

5. Am I taking responsibility for my life?

6. Am I living the life that I want?

7. Am I stuck in the patterns of my family and culture?

8. Am I afraid to get out of my familial patterns?

I would suggest that you continue writing in your journal as you go through this book and as well list and keep track of your negative and positive thoughts and feelings as you deconstruct your illusions—it's the story of you. One of the reasons that I find this to be important is that most of us do not realize how mired we are in negativity. I certainly didn't. I discovered that many of my thoughts were based in anger, fear, judgment, self-justification, depression, low self-esteem and sometimes even self-abuse—I wasn't even aware of it. Most of you will be shocked to see how many negative thoughts roam around freely in your psyche—and repeatedly—in your mind. One particularly difficult day I counted my negative thoughts and they were in the hundreds. It was shocking! The question is: Do you want to think like that? Negative thoughts are not going to make you a happy and vital person. Now we all have times in our lives when we are compromised and if this negative position continues for too long, then change is on the horizon.

When I asked Debbie if she was a happy person, she replied that she used to be but was now sinking into a deep depression because her relationship with her fiancé was on a downward spiral, exacerbated by his increasing mood swings. Even though she tried to work it out with him, he refused to make any changes or go to a psychologist or psychiatrist for consultation. Debbie realized that she had no choice but to end the relationship—a very difficult and painful decision because they had been together for eleven years. What made it worse was that she was very close to his mother and sister. The process of separating was not easy, but about six months later Debbie was in a new life, once again living authentically. She was no longer on depression medication and was waking up happy, like she used to as a teenager. Perhaps depression is the body's way of telling you that you are on the wrong track. Certainly Debbie found this to be true.

Another great thing about keeping a journal as you go through your change process is that years later, you can go back and reread what you wrote and remember what was churning in you emotional world at that particular time. As you continue processing the eight questions, explore these questions as well.

1. Do I choose to live the way my family wants me to live, or do I want to make another choice? *One client discovered that he did not want to take over his father's electrical company, even though he was the only son.*

2. Am I living the life that I want, or am I living someone else's dream? *Kayleen became a lawyer to please her parents, a story I discuss in the next paragraph.*

3. Am I anesthetizing myself with drugs and alcohol in order to deal with my reality? *My coworker told me that he was drinking in order to stand staying in his marriage.*

4. Am I in a job that is sucking the life out of me—a soul-crushing experience? *If you can't transform your relationship to your job as I did in my previous example, you need to have an exit strategy.*

5. Am I contorting myself to fit into a way of life that is not mine? *Nancy, a creative "free spirit," was trying to fit into the corporate world so that she could make a six-figure salary, but her plan was not working because she hated her job.*

6. What is not working in my life? *You need to be clear about the positive and negative aspects in your life and to make the desired changes.*

If you are resonating with any of these questions, perhaps it is time to take a conscious look at yourself and to tease out the qualities in yourself that you don't like from those that you do like.

The mirror exercise really affected Kayleen because she realized that she did not like herself, was unhappy, stuck, and not living the life that she wanted to live. She told me that when she initially looked at herself in the buff, she saw a lumpy, unattractive body belonging to an unhappy person. She hated herself and couldn't believe she had gotten to this place. Then she recounted what it was like going through the exercises, and the tears began to flow and then they morphed into those really deep soul sobs. She realized that no new set of clothing designed to hide all of her imperfections or no amount of money could change what was in the mirror. This exercise forced Kayleen to face a lot of personal issues as well as the fact that she was living her parents' dream. She hated practicing law, a familial career path that had begun with her great-grandfather, a renowned Supreme Court Judge. She went to law school to oblige her parents, both lawyers, because she was their only child. Now after practicing law for ten years, she felt like a shell of a person, was always depressed and on some sort of medication to numb her reality. She didn't want to live this life anymore and was having suicidal thoughts. This is what pushed her into therapy. In time and with a lot of therapeutic support, she changed her profession to that of an interior designer, which was very shocking to her family. With her creative side now engaged, Kayleen makes less money, is happier, and is no longer taking depression medicine or having suicidal thoughts. She is transforming her life and reclaiming her authentic soul-centered journey. Her parents were not happy about her choice to leave the revered law profession, but even they have acknowledged that she is happier. Kayleen continues to explore her creative side and feels like she is closer to her life's work and purpose. She doesn't know where she will end up, but she feels that her life is on track—her track—and not the track of her parents.

Parent Traps

After you take stock on a personal level, as Kayleen did, you must then begin peeling away the layers separating *what is yours* from *what is your parents*, in all areas. It is a complex process, but the following questions can serve as a "map" of the terrain:

1. What are the qualities of my mother and father that I like and want to cultivate?

2. What are the qualities of my mother and father that I dislike and want to eliminate?

3. With which of my parental values do I wish to align and which do I want to eliminate?

4. Do I like the relationship that my parents have (had) with each other?

5. Is this the kind of relationship I would want to create with my significant other?

Deconstructing parent traps is a totally unique process for each individual because everyone's life experiences are so varied.

Clearly there are many more questions that you can ask yourself. As you ask and answer the above questions think about other aspects, like:

1. Is my body in the shape of my mother or my father? Can I change that?

2. Do I talk like my mother or father?

3. Do I look like my mother or father?

4. Do I laugh like one of my parents?

5. Do I move in the world like either of my parents?

6. Am I clumsy, graceful, or athletic, like one of my parents?

Continue exploring all aspects of your parents and how they have affected your life. Journaling really helps to flush out perspectives you really never knew you had.

The other day I was watching CNN, and there was a daughter of a prominent family being interviewed. As I watched her speak, I became more and more horrified because she talked like, laughed like, and had the same ideas and perspectives as her mother—she was a mime of her family. There was no distinction, no authenticity, no self-perspective or soul development evidence. I wondered: Where is the *AUTHENTIC YOU* if your mother or father inhabits your body through voice, mannerism, ideology, and gesture? Where is the authentic self that needs to emerge, but can't. I am not saying that we shouldn't adopt familial patterns, but as adults we should become more conscious of what is ours and what is theirs. That is the process of becoming a healthy adult human being—a process of differentiation and conscious choice leading to variation.

Other Contextual Traps

After deconstructing the illusions of your parent traps, take a good look at the other aspects of your contextual factors such as siblings, relatives, friends, culture, community, career, religion, and work down the list. I have created a list of questions you can begin asking yourself, journaling your observations:

1. What qualities of my siblings do I like and dislike and how do they affect me?

2. What qualities of my relatives do I like and dislike and how do they affect me?

3. What qualities of my friends do I like and dislike and how do they affect me?

4. What qualities of my culture do I like and dislike and how do they affect me?

5. What qualities of my community do I like and dislike and how do they affect me?

6. What qualities of my career do I like and dislike and how does it affect me?

7. What qualities of my religion/spirituality do I like and dislike and how does it affect me?

Continue journaling and exploring your answers and don't be surprised if some of the answers are shocking. Also don't be afraid of straying beyond the familiarity of your contextual factors. Clearly there are millions of questions that you can ask yourself. I have only provided you with a start. Continue writing in your journal and dig in and dig deep because this is you doing your own analytical work to remove some of the veils of illusion that cover your soul. Remember that you can always keep the parts that you authentically want, like, and feel comfortable with, and leave the other parts behind. You can also add new parts, if you choose to, because it is a deeply personal journey without any roadmaps. You can drop one thing only to bring it back later.

Each individual has his or her own challenges. What is meaningful for one person may not be meaningful for another person because it is a unique process of discovery and choice. Nevertheless, you need to make choices and get clear about *who you are* and how you want to fit in to the world around you. It is

an exciting process of discovery! Making choices embraces creation energy—the creation of the authentic you living the life you
want. Unfortunately, sometimes people get stuck in a life that
they don't want because it is either dumped on them or they are
guilted into living that life.

Rashida's Story

A thirty-three-year-old Lebanese woman, Rashida, came into my
office and told me that she wanted a relationship with a man but
had to care for her parents because her brother and sister didn't
want that responsibility. She had become clinically depressed
because of the situation. She became the sacrificial lamb for her
family, who had dumped on her the burden of caring for the parents. Now there is nothing wrong with giving care to your family
members, but all siblings should participate in one way or another.
This case was very difficult and complicated and after getting the
family to agree to come in for some family sessions (which was a
miracle in itself) I was able to negotiate a reasonable distribution
of responsibility among the family members. The gift to Rashida
was that she was able to have a life and in time fell in love and got
married. The important point to remember is that if things are
unfair in your family life, you must be assertive and work to change
them. You must get help! Rashida did something that was out of
the box for her culture: she went to a psychologist for help, and she
got her life got back on track. She refused to be subservient and
moved out from her contextual factors and reclaimed her life. You
always need to make choices about the life you want to live.

Emily's Story

One of my patients, Emily, an only child, went to her cousin's
wedding whom she had not seen for twenty-five years (because
her parents died when she was fifteen and she was raised by a
family friend in another city). Before she left to go to the wedding, Emily reminisced about all the great times she and her
cousins had playing together at the family farm where they lived

and was very excited about reconnecting to her past. Now in her late forties, Emily was going through a difficult divorce and was finishing her PhD in anthropology so she could teach at a university, a childhood dream. When she came back, we processed her experience. She was shocked at her family's focus on materialism—they were overly concerned about where she lived in Los Angeles, what kind of a house she lived in, and where she sent her daughter to school. They were all a bit surprised to find out that she did not own her own home and sent her daughter to public school. Her familial contextual factors valued property and material achievements as a way of measuring personal success, rather than goodness, depth, spirituality, education, and living ones authentic soul journey. There was only one person at the wedding who had the ability to have an authentic conversation with Emily about her achievements, life experiences, and fulfillment of her childhood dream: her cousin's daughter who was recently diagnosed with cancer. I firmly believe this happened because this family's template of illusion (the contextual factors) was so strong and so constricted that they did not have the ability to even see my client's reality. They had no context in which to communicate to her except through their limited software.

Know Your Reality

People are defined by their contextual factors, and if something doesn't make sense to them, they simply don't understand it because they are operating from the perspective of their unconscious. It is this lack of perception, or perhaps constrained perception, that pushes people into a box that creates tunnel vision. Remember, *if you do not have the context to understand another person's reality, then you do not have the capacity to see what is in front of you.* To live a soul-centered life you must have the ability to open up your tunnel vision and create a consciousness that expands beyond the old templates. This is not a natural, organic process; it entails deep inner work. It is only natural to see what you have been programmed to see. In order to think differently, you need to move to the next level of consciousness and you have to think "out of the box" and commune with your Invisible Actor.

The story of going back to your original home is commonplace in the treatment room. I believe that going back to your past gives you an opportunity to see how far you have come in your own consciousness and understanding of life. The analysis of your qualities as well as your personal value system needs to be made multiple times during your life. I think it easier to see your growth and development when you address your past in some manner.

Exploration, separation, and differentiation are key individuation processes that we all employ when we deconstruct the illusions of our life because they take us beyond the boundary of our contextual factors. It is an intensely emotional process because it pushes us to explore new places in our psyche that we never imagined that we could go, but were inspired to go. During the deconstructing illusions phase the Invisible Actor moves to a place of alertness because the layers of the contextual factors begin to be peeled away one by one, making the soul more visible—an exciting process.

In order to answer the question *Who am I really?* and *Who am I becoming?* you need to deconstruct as many illusions as possible. Analyze your situation, know your reality and differentiate yourself from your contextual factors because this is the place where the individuation process and the archetype of transformation align. However, it takes courage to separate from the contextual factors that bind you and to trust the Invisible Actor as your guide. Mentors, psychologists, and teachers, can bring forth new ideas at this time and influence you as you to begin searching for answers to your life questions as well as owning the consequences of your actions. These individuals bring forth different perspectives with which you might beneficially align.

Mentorship

One way to notice the stirrings of the Invisible Actor is to have a mentor. Mentorship is one of the most underutilized resources available in the human experience. Mentors are important because they give you perspectives of life that are different from your family of origin.

They come in many forms: coach, friend, teacher, spiritual advisor, doctor, or even the next-door neighbor. Sometimes they just show up in your life, other times you seek them, or they could even be the result of a chance meeting. You may have one mentor or many and they may be around for a short time or a long time. However, they are critically important for your growth and development because they are different from your family and culture and therefore push you to grow and think differently. They help you to break from the limited belief systems of your family and create openings in your psychological framework. Mentors may also provide comparisons to your own contextual factors, which in turn open up greater possibilities for your life. Mentors contribute unknown experiences or perspectives, which may help to precipitate numinous, spiritual or miraculous experiences. Having mentors from different cultures, ethnicities, religions, philosophies, and societies can create greater depth, reduce limited thinking, and at the same time make your life choices and experiences very exciting.

My first significant experience with mentors were my modeling teachers because they took me out of my contextual factors and taught me about how to move about in the world with finesse. Besides teaching me how to sit, stand, and walk with elegance, they also taught me how to be a refined woman, who moves through the world with grace and dignity. My consciousness level increased from the knowledge and practice of all these new qualities because they were not a part of my family, being raised in a small farming community in Northern Canada. And when I had to deal with the tragic death of my brother Douglas, my modeling mentors were there to support and encourage me to be my emotional best, especially when I had to deliver a televised speech as Miss Edmonton, which I did with elegance and sincerity. I am deeply grateful for all they taught me.

My Mentor, Dr. Ng

Sometimes you choose mentors, and other times they just show up in your life and make a difference. One of these individuals was Dr. Ng, a Chinese acupuncturist, who began working out of our family business, a hotel in Edmonton, one week a month when I was about twenty years old. He was both culturally and medically different from anyone I had ever known. He stimulated my curiosity, so I hung around him whenever he came into town. One day he invited me to come in for an acupuncture session, so I did. It was a wild experience. He put needles all over my body, lit a small cigar-shaped bundle of healing herbs, and *smoked* each spot that held a needle. He told me the lit herbs would help make the needles more potent.

I watched, listened, and kept going back to see him every month. As part of my dietary prescription Dr. Ng took me off wheat, dairy, and red meat—this was radical for the mid 1970s but I did it, felt better, and looked better because of it. Every time he came into town I sat in his waiting room, talked to his patients, and became friendly with his secretary. I saw him cure some very sick people. One day his secretary told me her story: she was in a wheelchair for five years and that every doctor she went to told her she would never walk again—but Dr. Ng's treatment restored her ability to walk. This was my first experience of the miraculous, and it forever changed my relationship to traditional medicine and my choice of health care.

In a very quiet, subdued way Dr. Ng taught me about life, choices, and the power of healing. He knew I was emotionally struggling, he knew I was lost, and he knew that I didn't know what to do or where to go. He suggested that I become an acupuncturist; I told him that I didn't want to do that and what I really wanted to be was an actress. He then encouraged me to go for my passion. All the while, he just kept on gently teaching me about life, healing, and transformation. I watched him perform miracles on people—he was amazing! I remember sitting in his waiting room, talking to one of his patients who had been unable to conceive. After about six months of treatment he congratulated her on her pregnancy. She was thrilled and then later went to her medical doctor (who did not believe that she would ever be able to ever get pregnant) to do the blood tests, but they came back negative. Of course, when she returned the following month she told Dr. Ng of her disappointment, and he in turn told her that if he gives her another treatment she will have twins, to which she replied, great! The next month she came back and said that the blood tests were still negative and that she was definitely not pregnant, to which he replied, "You are pregnant," and asked her if she wanted triplets. She told him that she didn't care and that she only wanted to be a mom with healthy children. She returned for her next appointment one month later with the medical tests confirming that she was indeed pregnant with triplets. I met the triplets shortly after their birth—they were exquisite.

Dr. Ng never pushed his ideas on me but just let me be myself. One day he sat me down and told me that I had to move away from my family and go to Toronto to make it on my own. I was surprised at this because at that time I had never considered the possibility of leaving my family. That was a radical concept for me, but I later followed his advice. This is a poignant example of how constricted my contextual factors were.

When I was completing my degree in drama at the University of Alberta, I thought that my family name, *Oneschuk,* was too ethnic to be the name of an actress, so I asked Dr. Ng for guidance in helping me choose my new name. I knew that by changing my name, I was leaving my family history to become a creation of my own choosing. Dr. Ng and I both struggled with names, and it was not an easy process. After months and months of deep thought, he came up with the name of *Matthews*, after St. Matthew in the Bible. Since my original name, Selene, did not flow with Matthews, we both decided to go with the name *Selina Matthews*. My parents were not happy about my name change, but then again they were not happy about a lot of things that I had done in my life, so what was the difference.

Mentors Change Your Vision

Mentors give you a different perspective of the world and open doorways to new possibilities. Mentors help you to vision beyond your contextual factors and the illusions and patterns in which you were immersed at birth. They help you to change by providing a different structure and vision of what is possible. I invite you to go through the chapters of your life and remember your mentors, writing down how they influenced you. Writing their story of influence in your journal can lead to an amazing discovery.

CHAPTER 7

THE TRINITY MODEL

E ver since I was a child the number *3* has always been significant, but it wasn't until I became a psychologist that I understood why. The quintessential energy of three is known to foster spiritual growth and dynamic change, which is why I call this psychological theory *The Trinity Model*. Besides implying growth and movement toward wholeness, it is a symbol that resonates deep within my soul.

If we understand the five stages that underlie soul transformation and want to connect with the Invisible Actor, we also need to figure out the course of actions involved with living a healthy, soul-centered life. Many spiritual traditions have these actions built into their philosophies: There are the Ten Commandments in Christianity, the Five Vedic Principals in Hinduism, and the Five Pillars of Islamic philosophy.

I wanted to develop a psychological model that embraces the spiritual aspects of life in an uncomplicated and easy-to-understand manner. What emerged was—*The Trinity Model: Healthy Side, Shadow Side, and Divine Side*. This psychological model provides a way to analyze your life by categorizing aspects of your personality so that you can illuminate those aspects that may have been invisible to you. It also helps to put you on a path to living a soul-centered life by bringing visibility to the invisible aspects of your personality. Learning more about yourself and coming to an understanding of why you made certain choices in your life increases your level of consciousness. The Trinity Model may also bring into focus the entrapments of your contextual factors and how they facilitated your life choices, some of which you wanted and some of which you didn't. You will also get deeper answers to the questions of *Who am I?* and *What is my soul purpose?* In time you will create pathways that are authentically yours so that you can live the life that you want to live.

Healthy Side

By *Healthy Side*, I am referring to all the positive, transformational, forward-moving qualities that make you a good human being at home, at work and with your family in both the inner and outer life perspectives. By *inner perspective* I am referring to the favorable, productive and affirmative aspects of your character that you want the world to see and which may include qualities of loyalty, integrity, honesty, helpfulness, charitableness, consistency, good-heartedness, responsibility and accountability. From an *outer perspective* I am referring to the roles that you play such as being a good partner, parent, lover, and role model (professional, mentor, coach, father, mother) in the three large domains of your life: personal, career, and community at large. Blending all these into a healthy state of being is a clear boundary system and a stable character. Making a list of the positive qualities you embody will be helpful. Writing them down in your journal is a poignant experience that tells you *Who am I when I am in the Healthy Side?*

There is one quality I want to focus on by using a psychological lens—*integrity*— because of its depth and breadth of meaning in both our inner and outer worlds as well as its capacity to be experienced on both the positive and negative polarities. Integrity, as I understand it, is an ethical concept that emerges from consistency of actions in the areas of accountability, honesty, responsibility, and truthfulness. In other words, *what you say, you do!* This means that there is follow-though and congruency between your inner and outer perspectives. Integrity is a personal virtue that is aspirational. It incorporates your moral understandings and obligations and as well as your personal set of ethics. Integrity is related to your character. High integrity produces individuals who are whole, sound, morally upright, respected, and authentic. People with these qualities make excellent role models, mentors, and guides—that is, as long as they keep their Shadow Side in check.

Shadow Side

The *Shadow Side*, though often unconscious, is the dark and negative aspect of our personalities that we prefer to deny or keep hidden, such as our weaknesses, shortcomings, imperfections, immaturities, limitations, and other inferior characteristics. These repressed personal qualities can be very painful to deal with so we push them into the unconscious, an underground holding tank. This mechanism of repression is very complex, so you may need to get some assistance with a psychologist to maneuver through this material. Every human being has this side, though few want to admit it or even work on it. The concept of *shadow* was first articulated by Carl Jung.

Think about your life and journal about any shortcomings, impulsive behaviors, or indiscretions that you exhibited or that happened to you. Sometimes there are experiences that are kept hidden, like sexually abusing another or being sexually abused, that don't surface for twenty or thirty years. I have worked with many people with such buried experiences, and I can tell you it is never easy. Consciousness is a wake-up call!

I have organized the Shadow Side into three categories, which we all embody to varying degrees. They include:

1. Unhealthy negative emotions.

2. Unhealthy behavior patterns.

3. Unhealthy roles.

Unhealthy Negative Emotions

This first category of unhealthy negative emotions deals with emotions such as anger, rage, hatred, hostility, and sarcasm. These emotions can arise from life experiences wherein you were wounded, or they may have been assimilated from your contextual factors. Any psychologist will tell you that these negative emotions, if not detoxified or healed in some manner, can become precursors of illness or lead to negative behaviors in your relationships, career, and family settings.

Anger is just one example of a reaction to a distressing situation, usually one in which you feel repeatedly wounded. It is a complex emotion because it can be connected to childhood patterns and triggers negative emotions from past experiences. Even though anger has a positive function, I will only focus on the negative aspects. Anger can lead to physical violence, broken marriages/relationships, and addiction issues. Unfortunately, if your anger is not addressed, it can alienate others, impair judgment, disrupt lives, create unhappiness, and derail careers. Just think of all the movie stars, sports stars, and politicians who have fallen into this category. From a health perspective, people prone to anger and other negative emotions are at a higher risk for high blood pressure, heart disease, stroke, and weakened immune systems, so we must take these emotions seriously.

Unhealthy negative emotions not only affect you personally, but also those around you. It is important to journal and make a list of your negative emotions. If you can't think of any, just ask your friends and family, they will be happy to tell you—but I am warning you that you might not be happy to hear what they say! Remember negative emotions can come in many forms. Negative emotions can also lead to negative behaviors and patterns as in the example of Tony and Tina.

Tony and Tina's Story

Tony and Tina came into treatment to deal with Tina's complaints about her husband's sarcasm. Her husband did not think that his sarcasm was a big issue because he had grown up with it.

His parents had used sarcasm as a way to get a laugh. However, what this negative emotion did to his wife, who came from different contextual factors, was to erode her self-confidence and self-esteem—issues that then produced negative thoughts and behaviors toward her husband. This cycle did not lead to a happy marriage, which is why they were in my office. Once Tony became more aware of the consequences of his sarcastic comments, he worked on changing his familial patterns and the effect on his marriage was miraculous.

Unhealthy Behavior Patterns

This second category in the Shadow Side has two components—behaviors and patterns—which can be viewed separately, or together depending on the situation. *Unhealthy behaviors* reflect poor moral judgments that result in lying, cheating, stealing, and manipulating. These unhealthy behaviors stem from moral instability—a lack of integrity or dishonesty—and have a spectrum of consequences that can include everything from disruption of relationships to incarceration. These unhealthy behaviors can lead to unhealthy patterns such as physical abuse, and sexual abuse, to the hidden negative patterns of mishandling money or undermining a relationship. The more blatant the unhealthy behaviors, the easier they are to see; however, the less blatant forms are no less harmful. Often these "safer" unhealthy behaviors reflect a lack of integrity—the *what you say and what you do, don't match up problem*. Integrity, in its negative polarity, could manifest in something simple like "I'll call you tomorrow to set up a meeting" and then not doing it. Or it could come in the form of a commitment that you made to someone and then you don't follow.

Chantilly's Story

Chantilly was very much in love with a man who had asked her to marry him. She accepted his proposal on the condition that if they had any problems down the road, that they would go to therapy and work them out. He agreed wholeheartedly with this condition.

One year into their relationship, an impasse happened and Chantilly asked him to go to therapy. He agreed, so she made the appointment. At the last moment, he refused to go stating that he had done nothing wrong. In essence, his *not being a man of his word* ended the relationship. Her perspective was, if he was behaving this way before marriage, he would do it again during marriage. She could not trust him or respect him because he did not have integrity. Lack of integrity leads to numerous unhealthy behaviors and can destroy relationships and erode the respect that you had for your mate.

Alonso's Story

Alonso was having a series of affairs on his wife when she was unexpectedly diagnosed with cancer and died within a six-month time frame. He did not tend to her death or dying appropriately but continued philandering. Ten years later, he came into my office with severe clinical depression and was unable to work. Alonso did not understand why he was depressed because his life had been going well. His depression forced him to face some of his repressed Shadow issues, which included the shame, guilt, disrespect, selfishness, and immaturity he felt about his infidelity as well as not being present to his wife during her illness and death. His prior actions were now being handled via repression, and his feelings were surfacing in what seemed like an inappropriate time in his life, just before he was to marry another woman. However, he now had no choice. He had to do some deep inner work to reclaim his own health and come to terms with his prior unhealthy behaviors. *Shadow behavior is not free. It catches every one of us!*

Justine's Story

Justine was working on a project with a partner who professed integrity, stating that his word was "*as good as gold.*" Yet as their working relationship progressed, agreements that were made verbally and agreed upon by both parties were not honored in their legal documents. Her partner's words and actions did not match, as evidenced by the legal papers he insisted Justine sign. Hence she felt like she was working in quicksand. Needless to say, the project did not get off the ground because of his lack of integrity: The words and actions didn't share common ground. Perhaps his incongruent actions stemmed from unhealthy patterns learned from his family and cultural background. Integrity always leads to congruency between thoughts, speech, and action—*what you say, you do*—it is about honor. If you don't do what you say, then you are acting from your Shadow Side.

As an aside, every time that you say and do things that are not truthful, that are dishonest and lacking integrity, the negative actions you have put into play increase. In fact, the Shadow Side may even get so large that it will take over your Healthy Side and you wouldn't even know it. The paradoxical thing about the Shadow Side is that it feels very powerful even as it is eroding your self-confidence and self-esteem. You will get only an inflated sense of power (as easily deflated as a balloon) by degrading your true source of inner power because your Invisible Actor knows that you are not telling the truth. The only person you are cheating is yourself!

Unhealthy patterns as stated earlier may be learned behaviors that may have been created by your contextual factors, or by your personal experiences. I will provide you with a number of different examples. We all know people who fit into this category—however, in some cases it is hard to see.

Alex's Story

Alex was an Ivy League educated businessman who developed three separate businesses over the span of his career, and yet with all his credentials, all his businesses failed. Now at sixty-five years old he was losing his home. Somewhere in his psyche was a negative belief that his superior education provided him with all the tools he needed to run a business and therefore he didn't require any guidance or help from anyone. His failures were directly related to his contextual factors, as his father's business had also failed. The unfortunate thing was that he never chose psychological help.

John's Story

John had had a horrible childhood. He was beaten unconscious many times beginning when he was four years old. Most of these incidents happened when his father was drunk. When John got a little older, he was able to run to his grandparents' house three blocks away to get help. He would stay there until his father's alcoholic binge wore off. The next day his father always expressed remorse for his actions.

After John completed high school he left home to attend college in another city. He was doing well academically and eventually met Brandy, a fellow student, and fell in love. After six months, they ended up moving in together, and all was going well until they found out that Brandy was pregnant. Abortion was not an option for either one of them, so they had the baby. The stress of little money, trying to get good grades, and caring for a small baby boy was very difficult. Both John and Brandy seemed to be in a perpetual state of overwhelm. Even though John swore he would never hit anyone, he found himself physically acting out. He got mad one day and pushed Brandy into the wall and hurt her. John was ashamed that he was not able to control his violent impulses and subsequently started drinking, which exacerbated everything. One day after an intense argument the neighbors called 911, and John was hauled off to jail. This was a big wake-up call for him. He was court-mandated to attend Alcoholics Anonymous and anger management classes, as well as to attend individual psychotherapy. These three interventions saved John's life and the life of his family. Today John is a successful attorney with his marriage and family intact—a miracle. Never underestimate the power of the patterns of your contextual factors, and get help when you start to replay those behaviors or patterns.

It is important to journal about the negative behaviors and patterns in which you engage. Some of them may be learned from your contextual factors as in John's case. Get psychological help if you need to change some negative behaviors. *Knowing* what you are doing—however unpalatable—opens a door through which you can change your way of moving about in the world.

Unhealthy Roles

This third category in the Shadow Side includes a broad array of unhealthy roles that we can engage in depending on the situation that we are in. We usually engage these roles as a compensation for an insecurity that we are dealing with at that moment. Since we all have the capacity to engage in all these rolls, however briefly, the roles become a problem when we overuse them. The roles include the Trickster, Thief, Victim, Dissasociate, Narcissist, Saboteur, and Bully, to name a few. Each of these roles addresses a different aspect of the Shadow that comprises a spectrum of pathology. It is important to acknowledge that in some cases these roles may have a favorable or positive side; however, here I will focus only on the negative aspect.

Trickster Role

People who engage in the role of the Trickster enjoy breaking the rules and violating taboos—they cause discomfort in others while leaving themselves untouchable. Even though this role is all about personal gain, the main insecurity that is triggered is *feeling powerless.* This role runs the gamut from manipulating a situation, abusing power and lying about a situation to make the person look good all the way to total violation and corruption. Tricksters are clever, manipulative, and deceptive, using trickery and deceit as their defense. They come in many forms, like the stories about bosses who are abusive toward their employees while making themselves look indispensable to their employers, as an example. Recently, the Trickster role became shockingly visible in our popular culture with the demise of Bernard Madoff. He operated the largest Ponzi scheme in the history of America, pretending to be happy to see his friends and clients and at the same time stealing billions of dollars from them. Madoff is only one example: There are many others like him, big and small, who engage in the shadow behavior of the *Trickster*, as well as the *Thief*, which eventually leads to the ruining of their business and their incarceration. I would like to ask each of these people one question: *Was it worth it?*

Thief Role

When in the thief role you like to take things from others without asking—in fact you thrive on this quality. When you are in this role, however subtly your sense of integrity, morality, and ethics is skewed on the Shadow Side. The main insecurity that is triggered is a feeling of *lack* and *need*. This role encompass the entire spectrum of possibility from taking a pen, a lipstick, or an apple at the grocery store all the way to disarming alarms, picking locks, and opening safes. The shadow essence of this role is to be conniving and stealthy. You know when you have interfaced with people who are in this the role because as soon as they get what they want, they disappear. While shopping in the produce section of an organic grocery store I observed a short, chubby, man cautiously pick up an apple and begin eating it as he exited the store. He was not an employee.

Victim Role

Individuals engaged in the role of the victim like to blame others for the circumstances in their life because they are not able to take responsibility for their actions. This role triggers their insecurity of feeling *incapable* and *powerless* so they wallow in self-pity because their self-esteem is very low . . . they actually want people to feel sorry for them. The victim role can be anywhere on the spectrum from subtle to blatant. We can all engage in this role when we are going through dramatic changes in our lives and we need to bring consciousness to this. There is a specific version of this role that is rampant in our society at this time, the *Unworthy Victim*, but that will be discussed in another book.

Dissasociate Role

The Dissasociate role, on the other hand, avoids it all. When individuals are in this role, they *check out* and detach from their usual state. This role has a range of possibilities. On one hand, individuals in this role may have a sensation of being an outside observer because it is too painful to actually feel what is happening inside of them. On the other hand, they may just want to or choose to disconnect from the issues or person in front of them. The disassociate role can be learned in the family, or it can be a reaction to a family situation. It can also be the result of a traumatic situation or series of traumas. When people engage in the Dissasociate role, their insecurity triggers a deep intrinsic fear that they are *not good enough* or *strong enough* or *interested enough* to face what is happening to them, which is why they disappear. This role may be a precursor for addictive behaviors. The Disassociate role is becoming more and more prevalent in our culture with the increasing dependence on social media, because we check out of the human connection to connect with others via technology.

Marlena was fourteen years old when her Uncle Ted tried to kiss her. This was shocking to her! She immediately told her mother, and as a result Uncle Ted was never again allowed to come over to their house. Her mother thought that removing Uncle Ted from their life would resolve everything because nothing had actually happened. However, that was not the case. Anytime Marlena went near older men, even if they were teachers or coaches, she would shrivel up and take on a vacant look. Her homeroom teachers noticed the change in her behavior and informed her mother. Simultaneously Marlena began to gain weight and wear baggy clothes, and these new behaviors worried her mother. This was not how she had acted before the incident, which is why she brought her in to see me.

Marlena's fearful reaction to her uncle was causing her to "check out." She felt betrayed and unsafe. It took a lot of time for Marlena to feel secure within herself and not to check out. We spent many hours processing her fear and anxiety as well as strengthening her boundary system, her self-esteem, and her confidence so that she would not have to disappear in order to be around men. I am grateful that her mother was astute enough to get help. Eventually Marlena was able to be around men of any age and not fade away. Unfortunately, many people don't take these traumas and negative experiences seriously, and they think that because someone is young, he or she will either grow out of it or else time will heal the wound. This is an illusion.

Narcissist Role

When we engage the Narcissist role, we are in a me-centered state where we require excessive admiration. We feel special and strive for attention at this time. We need the external world to reflect us at this time because what is triggered is a *lack of confidence and self worth* in our own resources, our insecurity. The Narcissist role goes the gamut of occasional to severely pathological. When we engage this Narcissist role, however slight, we are operating from a distorted worldview and are completely unconscious of this aspect. We can have aspirations of glory and need to feel superior at this time, but unfortunately this superiority is only an illusion. People tend to think of us as aloof and insensitive during these times. This role also makes us hypersensitive to criticisms and the judgments of others.

Saboteur Role

The *saboteur* is one role with which we all have to deal, to a greater or lesser degree: a gremlin, a shadowy entity that lives in each of us and that stands in the way of change in both our personal and professional life. The *Saboteur* uses negative thinking to cast self-doubt and shame on our parade, making endless ruminations about our situation. The saboteur is triggered by our low self-esteem and self-worth, so it *criticizes* us in order to further sap our energy and reduce our sense of self. The Saboteur stops us from having the success that we really want and deserve. In order to go forward toward change, you must reduce the size of your Saboteur, the primary defender of the unhealthy status quo.

Frank was a graphic designer who was getting a lot of acclaim for his work. However, in the dating department he was failing miserably. Every time he would get close to asking a girl out, he would start sweating and go through a barrage of negative thoughts, like *I'm not good enough, I'm too heavy,* and *I'm not successful enough so why would she even go out with me?* He sabotaged himself from getting into a relationship with the girl of his dreams. The goal of the inner Saboteur is to make you fail at a task, experience, or undertaking, so you must get control of that role in order to have a healthy life. If you find yourself in this role often, you may need to consult with a psychologist to get help.

Bully Role

When we are in the role of the bully we use aggressive behavior to intentionally hurt another person emotionally, verbally, or physically so that we can gain power over him or her. When engaged in this role we lack compassion and empathy and feel no remorse for our actions, because we are immersed in the Shadow Side. The insecurity that is triggered is one of *being powerless,* so we compensate by needing to control something or someone. The bully role tends to direct its abusive behavior toward others whose race, religion, gender, sexual orientation, or ability level triggers the abusive behavior. People who physically abuse others are engaged in this role, and this can include everything from men who batter women all the way to teens who bully their peers. Recently this role of the bully has become a nationwide concern in response to the number of teenagers that have committed suicide—now termed "bullycide." The stories are tragic! The role of the Bully must be taken seriously because it can lead to the death!

The Gifts of Shadow Work

Confronting shadow material requires courage, fearlessness, true grit, and tenacity. It is one path that can that lead to the illumination of your own eternal flame, the Invisible Actor within. Clearly, Shadow Side problems are prevalent in our culture—just look at the politicians, actors, and religious teachers whose careers have been completely destroyed because of their Shadow Side. In order to participate in soul transformation, you must both expose and work through your Shadow Side. A person who continually works with his or her Shadow Side will become more whole, with an open mind and heart, and subsequently will live a deeper, richer, and more conscious life. This individual will have the dignity of knowing that he or she did the psychological work necessary to make conscious choices and take responsibility for his or her actions and life trajectory.

Going through the three categories of the Shadow Side and journaling about your traits is an illuminating process. By writing in your journal you will answer the question, *Who am I when I am in the Shadow Side?*

Reworking your unhealthy emotions, behaviors, patterns, and roles shifts you to the positive and Healthy Side of life. Before you rework anything through you must accept the software operating system that you have. When attempting psychological change, you want to look at it from a number of different angles—be a detective. Be clear which aspect you want to change. Write it down and focus, seeing your past indiscretions for what they were—unconscious choices—and now you are ready to make a conscious choice to change using the *Four-Part Process of Change*. Bring consciousness to one aspect at a time, so as to not feel overwhelmed.

Four-Part Process of Change

The process of changing unhealthy emotions, behaviors, patterns and roles to positive ones is a four-part process. You can indeed try the process by yourself by following the four steps but be sure and seek psychological help if you start to feel shaky or overwhelmed.

1. Decide on the one thing that you want to change right now and bring your full awareness to it. Lets use sarcasm as an example.

2. Try to stop the remark or behavior before it happens.

3. When you hear yourself or feel yourself being sarcastic try to stop the sarcastic remark from coming out of your mouth. Hold it in your mind. The first few times you will not catch yourself till after you have said it. However, with time and perseverance, you will eventually catch yourself halfway through saying the sarcastic remark.

4. Catch the remark or behavior midstream, apologize and then restart the behavior.

5. When you catch yourself being sarcastic, even in the middle of a sentence, stop, apologize, and then restart the behavior and sentence again correctly. With practice, you will eventually catch yourself before the sarcastic word or behavior comes out of your mouth.

6. Recreate and revision positive Healthy Side words and behaviors. Replace the sarcastic word with a positive word or action.

This is very much a psychological process that you can work through on your own, one day at a time. Remember, real change is subtle and not linear. Psychological reworking is a slow process that needs to happen continuously throughout the lifespan. You are in charge of your own life, so perhaps you should imagine reworking your software system as if you were running your own business—you are the CEO of your life.

One of the consequences of change is that you might lose some old friends, but know that you will gain new ones. Losing friends is not an easy process, but sometimes a necessary one on the road of life. You can never change who you are. All you can do is bring consciousness to who you are and make different choices. Some people can transition with you to new levels of consciousness, and some can't, so you need to make choices and move forward. The deeper and more connected you are to your body and soul, the greater your level of consciousness. Moving forward to Healthy and Divine Sides will change the direction and future of your life, and as a result, you will be happier.

Divine Side

By *Divine Side* I am referring to the part of our self that is aligned with our soul, the Invisible Actor within. This side has the capacity to unite your inner divinity with the outer cosmic divinity giving you a deep connection to an energy that is beyond you. This side inspires your spiritual practices of prayer, ceremony, and rituals, which can ground you. Many spiritual traditions prescribe ways to live life that inspire divine consciousness. However, if you wish to create your own spirituality and connection to the Divine, you can do so by integrating aspects from both formal and informal traditions, including everything from mediation, mindfulness, and breathing techniques, to facilitate the process of engaging the Invisible Actor.

The Divine Side also embraces the unordinary experiences of the spiritual and the miraculous as well as the numinous experiences that erupt unexpectedly out of body and soul, because they are all connected to the divine spiritual power that lives within your soul. From an everyday perspective this side may comprise your dreams, the synchronicities you experience, your relationship with nature, and the artistic images that transform you. This divine side is intimately connected with the hero and heroine's journey.

Write down in your journal the manner in which you connect with the divine so you can know *Who am I when I am in the Divine Side*? When you know and understand how you connect with the Divine, the Invisible Actor becomes fully engaged in its covenant: taking you to higher levels of consciousness.

Analyze Your Life

The Trinity Model gives you an uncomplicated method with which to analyze your life and make choices about how you want to live. Journal and explore yourself and your actions in each category. It is a fascinating process! However, if you are struggling with a few of these concepts, go to a psychologist to get help. The Healthy and Divine Sides are fairly straightforward to analyze and write about, but the Shadow Side is very tricky. Continue questioning yourself and your level of integrity. Also know the roles that you use to get what you want. Be truthful. The level of authenticity of your perception is a choice, and each choice has a perspective and consequence. The more we understand about *the good, the bad, and the ugly,* the higher will be our consciousness. Besides going through each of the three Shadow categories, figure out how much time you spend in each one . . . interesting information. The focus of the Trinity Model is to bring awareness to the *inner trinity* that lives within your body, voice, and soul.

The goal of The Trinity Model is to facilitate individuation and help you to become an authentic, soul-centered human being by making choices about your life, taking responsibility for those choices, and working towards increasing your consciousness by "growing up" the Healthy and Divine Sides of your personality and "growing down" the Shadow Sides. It is all about making authentic choices. The authentic you can only know itself by going through a process of separation and distinction. This knowledge allows you to live a healthy, soul-centered life.

CHAPTER 8

CHOICE AND FREE WILL

ife is all about making a series of choices. You may not like the choices that you have in front of you all the time, but you have a choice about the way that you wish to run your life. Some of the choices may be easy, whereas others challenging, sending you on a path that is different from your contextual factors and life as you know it—a road rarely traveled. You are the CEO of your life, and you must take that role seriously. All the choices that you make are based on your values, intellect, judgment, perceptions, intelligence, illusions, psychological insights, and personality structure. The Trinity Model assists you in becoming even more conscious about your choices. The great thing about choice is that it gives you the freedom to open avenues to new dimensions of experience in the world. You always will have a choice because you were born with the supreme and awesome capacity of *free will*. With free will as your rudder you can choose your life: one of confinement and shackles or one of growth and possibility.

Free will is an extraordinarily complex and multi-dimensional concept that philosophers and religious scholars have written about and fought over for centuries. I can only illuminate my understandings of free will through my psychological lens and contextual factors. I define *free will* as an ability to choose an action or course of actions in order to fulfill a personal desire for which you take responsibility, both consciously and unconsciously. Clearly, illusions and projections about your contextual factors and emotional attachments to them will affect your capacity to engage your free will. However, I would like you to consider *choice as freeing your will from the entanglement of those attachments.* Free will holds you accountable for your choice of actions throughout your life and is connected to your level of consciousness and intelligence. Clearly, free-will life choices can be made on the Shadow Side, Healthy Side, or Divine Side of life. I provide you numerous examples of free will choices from both a relational and individual perspective.

Omar's Story

Omar, a young Egyptian man, was so heartbroken that his entire body shook with the grief as his tears poured like little rivers down his cheeks. Now we have all gone through breakups, and we all know how painful the process is. Omar's story is reflective of many cultures: Lebanese, American, Russian, Chinese, Persian, Ukrainian, Jewish, Egyptian and German. Omar fell in love with a beautiful massage therapist, Angelina, with whom he had been dating for six months and wanted to marry. The time came to tell his parents about the serious nature of his relationship and to make the appropriate introductions. Omar told his parents about Angelina, but they refused to even meet her because of her profession, referred to her as a whore who goes to other men's homes to give them a massage and whatever else they wanted. Omar's parents then made it very clear that neither they, nor their affluent community, would accept her. Omar's parents were reacting from their family, culture, and community contextual factors. Change for them was not an option, because they were operating from a constricted position.

Love is an emotional attachment energy. Heartbreak is the suffering caused by the breaking or pulling apart of that emotional attachment energy—an excruciatingly painful process in which the soul weeps. It is no surprise that the classic symbol for love is the thorned rose. If love is an attachment, energy then nonattachment energy is a transcendent energy, the realm of unconditional love. Clearly, there are different levels of love and the deeper the love attachment, the more unbearable the process. What actually breaks in the love relationship is the illusion of attachment because *what you imagined can no longer be.* You may be able to transform the situation, but the illusion of what was will never be what it once was. Love is a constant flow of being pulled together and then pulled apart—it is a magnetizing energy.

Omar can make many choices given his heartbreaking dilemma, but I will explore only four possibilities to give you a deeper understanding of a free-will choice. The process of choosing comes with its own set of consequences: rewards and punishments. Free will is your rudder, maneuvering you strategically around the illusions and attachments you encounter so that you can make the best choice for yourself—one with which you can live. For example, if Omar chooses to breakup with Angelina and listen to his parents and marry someone whom they will accept, he is choosing to attach to the illusion of his family's contextual factors rather than his beloved. If Omar is truly in love with Angelina, he will pay a heavy price emotionally—*heartbreak*—meanwhile, his parents will be exempt from paying any price. The problem is when you do something solely to placate the family, you disconnect from your heart and soul. The consequence of this choice will likely lead Omar to a state of depression, despair, and hopelessness—it is inevitable. For some people this despair will happen immediately and for others it will be a slow calculated burn that turns to anger, rage, and then hatred. By ending his relationship with Angelina, Omar would keep his family's contextual factors and illusions alive, and in the process, forfeit his ability to fully engage his masculine power and be a man—a huge price to pay.

However, if Omar decides to follow his heart and marry the love of his life, his soulmate—walking away from his family, breaking his contextual factors, and taking responsibility for his own life and future family—he would take on the consequences for his actions. However, Omar would also be heartbroken with this choice because of his emotional attachments to his family. What he would actually be doing is choosing one form of heartbreak over another. Clearly if he chooses this path it is a more difficult journey, but one that is empowering for him because he becomes a man in control of his own "castle" and destiny, his reward. History provides us many examples, but the one that I find most fascinating is Britain's King Edward VIII who abdicated his throne to marry Wallis Simpson, a divorced American woman and the love of his life.

A third possibility is that Omar goes to a psychologist to help him process his difficult dilemma. Going to a professional to get help is very important because he or she is trained to *not* get caught up in your contextual factors nor to be attached to the outcome. The job of psychologists is to give you options and process the possible consequences of the choices you are considering. Talking with your friends and family does not work because they are caught up in your attachments and contextual factors, and most of the time they do not have the psychological education, or therapeutic tools, to guide you. They may be amazing individuals, but they are untrained and not always cognizant of the long-term consequences of your possible choices. Perhaps engaging an Egyptian psychologist might be another choice to find a middle ground, a circumstance with which both Omar and his family could live. In therapy, *all* possibilities should be considered.

The fourth choice would be to surrender. Surrendering allows you to the time to engage with your Invisible Actor, which should always be the first choice when difficult situations arise, but it seldom is. When you surrender, you must be silent, meditate, do your spiritual practices, regroup, perhaps go somewhere in nature where you can listen to your inner voice and dreams and wait till a deeper truth about your situation is illuminated. Sometimes the process takes time, but if you wait long enough, you will get your answer. When you are in this surrendering space, do not pray or meditate for certain outcomes to occur because you will only engage your illusions. Instead, be nonattached—be open to any and all possibilities. Ask yourself:

1. Why has this dilemma been brought to me?

2. What is the deeper meaning of this situation?

3. What is the higher good that can come from this?

Making your choice from this perspective brings you closer to your Invisible Actor, your soul guide. Surrendering to your Divine Side allows for the play of reality to move forward, rather than the play of illusion to move forward. A poignant lesson that every human being must learn is this: *Your soul is greater than your contextual factors because it is the hard drive and not the software operating system.*

Dallas's Story

Every family has their culture-based level of tolerance for unique and different situations. Dallas, a twenty-nine-year-old nurse whom I had already been seeing for two years, told me about a medical technician who had asked her out on a date. She said that he was really cute, but that he was Muslim. Their relationship developed slowly, and in time they fell in love. Even though there were a lot of cultural and religious issues that needed to be worked out, they seemed open to making their relationship work. They regularly practiced their respective faiths, Christian and Muslim.

When the time came for Dallas to tell her parents about Mohamed, she became very anxious because he was a devoted Muslim who prayed five times a day. She was also very concerned that Mohamed would dump her if he found out that she had been previously married—a mistake about which she was ashamed. However, I encouraged her to tell him the truth about her previous marriage. It was tense between them for a while, but they eventually worked things out. Dealing with all the cultural and religious, issued not to mention past indiscretions, is never easy, but the two of them managed to accomplish this. Mohamed's mother took a liking to Dallas and taught her how to prepare some of Mohamed's favorite traditional meals, which she also had begun to enjoy. Clearly a lot of integration and collaboration occurred from both sides of the family.

After a year of dating Mohamed, Dallas came in for a session and showed me her beautiful engagement ring. She told me that their parents had met and were respectful of each other because they could see the love between their children. These two culturally different families had a quality of openness and a readiness for change; they were embodying the Healthy Side of life. Dallas and Mohamed were both surprised at their parents positive responses to their differences and began to have a deeper respect for both of their families. Their parents, in contrast to Omar's parents who focused on themselves and their extremely divergent contextual factors, focused on helping their children create a healthy, integrated, multicultural, and multireligious home.

Before Dallas and Mohamed got married, they dealt with their hot-button topics such as which holidays they were going to celebrate, how they were going to raise their children, and if Dallas was going to convert to Islam. They both agreed that their children would be raised Muslim, but that they would also be exposed to other religions including, Christianity and Buddhism. Dallas decided that she would not convert, but would respect all the Muslim holidays and traditions. Three years after our last therapy session, I saw Dallas at the mall pushing her six-month-old son, looking as happy and radiant as ever. All was going well in her life, and I was thrilled for her. Couples coming together from diverse backgrounds bring so much flavor to their relationships and families. Multicultural families anchored in the Healthy Side of life bring depth, capacity, and collaboration—the richness of difference.

Scott's Story

Sometimes life puts us into situations where we may have to make a freely willed choice between two bad choices. When I was in the early stages of studying psychology, I thought that such a dilemma would almost never happen. My naivety! It also happened to me!

Scott told me about Sheena, a woman with whom he was very much in love. They met at Starbucks one morning as they were getting their lattes. She was from a prominent family but he was not. In time having fallen in love, they wanted to marry. Sheena's parents forced her to present Scott with an unfair prenuptial agreement, which drastically limited Scott's equality ability to be a partner to Sheena for their entire marriage. In fact, Scott was completely thrown off balance when he read the agreement. He was now faced with a dilemma that he found to be unsettling. He had to then make a choice between signing an agreement that devalued him and that he did not agree with, so that he could marry his love or else end the relationship. He weighed his options: If he married the women he loved, he would have a better life, and it would be easier for him to complete his degree in architecture and begin his business, versus not getting married to the love of his life, being alone, and struggling to complete his education, but remaining true to himself and his values. After giving the two options a lot of thought, he decided to sign the agreement. Scott was a romantic and believed in love and thought that love could overcome any difficulty. In his heart he knew that he loved Sheena and was not after her or her parents' money. What he was unaware of was that Sheena's constricted contextual factors were operating right from the beginning of their relationship and as well as in their prenuptial agreement, which legally defined the nature of their relationship. Seven years later, because of the intense dysfunction of his in-laws, along with Sheena's inability to maintain appropriate boundaries with her family, the marriage failed.

When I processed the story with Scott, he still maintained that he had made the best decision because he was now a very successful architect. However, he never attempted the third or fourth options: He never processed his situation psychologically or spiritually, so that he could reframe his situation, nor did he surrender to the experience to find out what the lesson was for him or what the higher purpose of this situation was. Not always is the road of life easy, sometimes you just have to make the best choice from the cards that you were dealt—take your hits and move forward. However you should contemplate at least four types of choices:

1. Process option one.
   In Scott's case, he had to decide if he was going to sign the unfair prenuptial agreement and marry the love of his life, which would lead to an easier life financially, but he would have to live with his personal value system devalued.

2. Process option two.
   In Scott's case, if he was unable to sign the unfair prenuptial agreement, he would have to end his relationship, and struggle financially to complete his education, but he would have remained true to his personal value system and integrity.

3. Reframe the situation.
   In Scott's case, he never processed the situation with a psychologist to give him a broader understanding of the consequences of either of his choices or other options.

4. Surrender to the situation.
   In Scott's case, he did not surrender to the experience and listen to a voice deep within or even find out what the higher meaning of this situation was.

When you follow these four steps, you will learn a lot more about yourself, your situation, your character, as well as build your courage bank, your inner strength, and your connection to the Healthy and Divine Side of life. In whatever freely willed choice you make, you must always do it with integrity. Take the high road, even if you don't want to. *Integrity costs*—but it is always the best choice because it has the least baggage.

Melinda's Story

In the therapy room I have worked with a lot of people facing personal dilemmas, and one thing that I have learned is this: When an individual makes a freely willed choice, he or she takes responsibility for it and owns the consequences. Melinda was referred to me by an orthopedic doctor because of her psychological symptoms resulting from a repetitive stress injury: severe depression, panic attacks, debilitating pain, and insomnia. After assessing her psychological state and processing her options, I suggested that she take a minimum of six months to one year off. She told me that she did not want to do that because she wanted to pay her mortgage and continue sending her child through college.

As a psychologist I always find it difficult to watch someone abusing his or her body physically or emotionally, for however the noble the cause. However, I tried to find a middle ground with Melinda, to suggest ways she might lessen the stress on herself, but she was locked in her stance, and I could not find the right key. I decided to let her know what I foresaw as the consequences of her decision once again and reframed her situation: If she did not take time off, she might cripple herself and end up on disability. I also encouraged her to surrender and listen to a voice deep inside to help guide her.

Melinda could not hear me; instead she rattled on that she was willing to sacrifice herself because she didn't want to lose her house. Melinda was dealing with an attachment to responsibility—her attachments were to her home and putting her kids through college. She was also strongly attached to her identification as the provider, the one who could shoulder all the burdens for the sake of home and hearth. In other words Melinda was attached to her sense of herself in the role of the provider, rather than being attached to her body, the home of her soul. There were times when I saw her in such excruciating pain that I didn't know how she was functioning, but she just kept on bulldozing through. Unconsciously what she was saying was that she was willing to sacrifice her body, her physical well-being, for money to keep the illusion of her contextual factors alive.

This is a common mistake, especially for women. How many of you have sacrificed your body to keep your illusion alive? I suspect many of you. Melinda was so wrapped up in her fear about her finances that she could not admit the seriousness of the depression, pain, and panic attacks she was experiencing, or even think about any other alternative for meeting her life's needs. Her finances were intricately connected to her contextual factors—the illusions, by which she was blinded. Actually, for many of us, financial problems are an eye-closing issue. Melinda's freely willed choice was located in the Shadow Side of her personality. There was another alternative or choice that she did not see. Losing her home over losing her body is a choice between two negative situations.

Even though I did everything that I could to bring consciousness to the situation, Melinda made excuses and was inconsistent with her therapy. She wanted to do things her way—the way of her engrained contextual factors—of which she was unconscious. She was not willing to surrender or to the process or ask herself the hard questions: *What is the deeper meaning of this situation in my life?* And, *What do I need to learn from this?* Nor did Melinda reframe her situation as an opportunity for growth, but instead remained stuck in the illusion of her contextual factors. She was unable to go to the Healthy Side and experience this situation as an opportunity, such as using this difficult life situation to teach her children how to transcend difficult situations, as well as transcend the limits of negative attachments.

Well, six months later, after missing another series of appointments, Melinda came in because her condition had deteriorated. She told me that I was right, but that she wanted to work only for six more months to finish paying her back taxes, and then she would leave her job. What could I say; she didn't get the spiritual lesson that the Invisible Actor was giving her. She made her choice, once again, an old familial pattern, to place her attachment toward responsibility and money ahead of her attachment to her body. Unfortunately, she was only able to work for three more months before she ended up on complete disability with the reality of foreclosure haunting her. When I saw her for the final session, she took responsibility for her choice and decision, told me that I was right, that she should have taken at least the six months off, gave me a hug, and moved on in her life. Free will gives you the freedom to choose the direction of your life, but you must be aware of your options and take them seriously. Who am I to judge Melinda's choice? It was her soul journey, not mine and we *always* learn, even if we never make a single change.

Attachments and Illusions

An attachment to anything is an illusion, whether it be your contextual factors, the pleasure of the reward, the fear of punishment, the mantle of responsibility, or even to physical objects such as your iPhone. We are all greater than our attachments and illusions. An aspirational goal for each of you is to free yourselves from as many attachments, illusions, and projections of your contextual factors as possible, which in turn will give you a greater sense of freedom and ability to make freely willed choices. This is not an easy task, because we are all attached to something. I deal with my own array of attachments daily. When you come from a perspective of freely willed choice, you are present with yourself, in the *here and now* state, and you are in control of your life and destiny.

CHAPTER 9

CONVERSATIONAL ILLUSIONS

onversations are just one way that we exchange information. We also gather information by watching television, listening to the radio, viewing movies, reading magazines, surfing the Internet, bloging, texting, and tweeting. I want to bring attention to how all these aspects affect the way that you communicate because the styles you use illuminate the illusions with which you are engaged.

The other night I went to a dinner party that included friends and their children who were in their twenties and thirties, a formal sit-down dinner with fifteen guests. After we were all seated I noticed that that there were three cell phones at the table belonging to the twenty-and thirty-year-old crowd. I noticed that they discretely answered their texts as they were eating and conversing with others. Social media has infiltrated dinner tables not only with my friends but with people all over the world. Later on I even brought out my iPhone, checked my messages, sent a few texts, and then showed the hostess, a wedding photographer, the pictures for the cover of this book to get her take on which picture that she thought I should use. Social media has forever changed the way we communicate and amass information.

Even though there are many types of conversational styles that are part of our daily lives, whether we are talking or texting, social media exacerbates this feeling of disconnection because it engages us in the role of the Dissasociate—we remove ourselves from the human experience and *check out* even if it is only for a minute. In terms of normal conversation, do you know how you manage your conversations with people on a daily basis? Do you talk *at* someone? Do you talk *to* someone? Do you talk *around* someone? Do you talk *over* someone? Or do you use a combination of types? And what does your style say about you?

The manner in which we communicate information is under our personal control. You need to assess which conversational style you use, along with the type of illusion that is attached to it. Becoming more conscious of how you communicate is one way that you can choose how you want to live your life. The more we increase our understanding of how we communicate, as well as the consequences of the style and the illusion it fosters, the greater will be our ability to live a soul-centered life.

I have created seven conversational styles to help you become more aware of the illusions that you use to communicate with others: Jumping Jack, Diplomatic, Unloading, All about Me, Fad, Gossip, and Communing.

Seven Conversational Styles

1. *Jumping Jack Conversations*

Jumping Jack Conversations contain information that is thrown around, jumping from topic to topic. This style is all about *talking around* another person and not to him or her. During one of my lunch breaks I observed two women, Mia and Nikki, at the table next to me. Mia talked about what had happened on the *Jimmy Fallon Show* last night while Nikki responded by telling her about her latest Internet date. Mia then changed the direction of the conversation (while she was texting and tweeting) to her mother coming to spend the weekend with her. Nikki replied by saying that she wanted to go shopping to buy some new shoes.

Clearly these two women are in a conversation, and information is shared between them in a free-flow manner—but it is disconnected and unrelational, which leads to a shallow me-centered style that seems to be socially and culturally acceptable at this time. This interaction style perpetuates self-centered and narcissistic behaviors because the *other* is never seen or "witnessed," which unconsciously increases isolation and exacerbates painful illusions of separation. Sharing information without the investment of the self is ultimately isolating and unsatisfying. Perhaps this conversational style reflects how isolated and disconnected we are as a society despite all the technological advances that connect us on a daily basis.

2. Diplomatic Conversations

We have all gone to formal events where we have had to behave in an *proper* manner, and I can tell you from my own experience that I find these sort of events to be very stuffy and superficial. In these situations I often have thoughts of acting out in some inappropriate manner, but I have so far been able to control myself and not let my Shadow Side take over.

Diplomatic Conversations are all about being polite, as well as being socially and politically correct, but they are essentially conflict-avoidance exercises. This conversational style engages a more superficial side of our personality because there is a concern or fear, either real or perceived, that we may hurt, reject, insult, offend, or be abusive to someone if we are not sensitive to the needs of the *other* or situation, in their manner of speaking. In this conversational mode the authentic self or truth is never spoken, and the absence of this authenticity unconsciously exacerbates a negative and non-productive illusion. Individuals in this circumstance may have the desire to connect, but their situation prevents them from doing so, leading to frustration. This style is essentially dissatisfying because we are holding back who we are, politically and culturally to fit in socially. It is an illusion of civility because it is a compromised position. It is also very isolating because we have to hide who we really are.

3. Unloading Conversations

Unloading Conversations are all about dumping your bubbling-up emotional angst onto someone else so that you can feel better. The other day I was standing at Whole Foods, an organic grocery store, waiting to pay for my groceries, and this women just began unloading, a very sad story of her life, using me as her receptacle. I am grateful that I knew what she was doing and that I could help her process her anger and rage, even if it was for a three-minute session. I paid my grocery bill, thinking that I should send her a bill, when she thanked me for listening to her and told me that she felt better for "letting it out." I was grateful for the acknowledgment and just moved on in my day, thinking that I had done a good deed.

Unloading conversations are a me-centered method of spewing negative illusions at other people to process anxiety because we don't want to process it ourselves. We all do this from time to time. It is considered to be a more primitive form of communication because we are *talking at* someone. In essence, we use others as a garbage disposal because we are not able to process the information in our me-centered stance. The problem with using this conversational style is that our issues will continue to resurface, and we will continue to unload onto others, until we do your own personal work. Just think about how often you use this style with your friends.

4. All-About-Me Conversations

Have you ever met someone who talks incessantly and you can't get a word into the conversation no matter what you do? Even though All-About-Me Conversations may not be as common as some of the other styles, you know them when they hit you because you feel like you are getting a barrage of vocal bullets. Individuals who engage in this conversational style are a both *talking at* you and *over* you. These individuals are in a severe unconscious illusion of desperation and isolation. Perhaps they are loquacious because they have an unconscious need to take control of the conversation as a defense against their low self-esteem. Talking makes them feel good about themselves. What matters is how you are affected. It is best to keep strict boundaries when you find yourself in such a situation because this type of conversation is a source of drain with no gain.

5. Fad Conversations

If you want to be hip and cool and part of a scene. you will want to engage in this type of conversational illusion. Fad Conversations tend to be superficial because they engage in an illusion through the use of mimicry—the opposite of authenticity. Fad conversations are preset styles of conversation that someone else created and that you want to be a part of. In essence they are already illusory making them a double illusion. Individuals engaged in this conversational style are in an unconscious illusion of desperation and isolation and even though they have a desire to connect. The problem is that they don't connect because they do not have any relationship with their authentic self; they are borrowing a lingo and attitude to feel connected to a group. Individuals that tend to be engaged in these type of conversations embrace me-centered perspectives and attitudes that are culturally driven. This conversational style may be more common with young people as in "valley girl" talk, and "rap" lingo: however, I have seen it in adults as well.

6. Gossip Conversations

We all gossip to some extent, whether we admit it or not. Gossip has become a trillion dollar business if you consider all the magazines and television shows that use this type of communication style. As I was writing my dissertation and intensively studying Jung, Dante, and Shakespeare, I was reading sleazy tabloid magazines on my lunch breaks. Then I discovered, to my surprise, that many other fellow students were engaged in this same behavior. Perhaps the polarities of intellect and gossip were needed to create balance.

Gossip Conversations happen everyday, everywhere, in our personal, and professional lives. They are all about illusory pre-occupations with *others*, on a small scale with our friends, relatives, and coworkers, and on a global scale with the celebrities. By talking about the events and situations of *others* we get to explore our own lives, or lack of them, as well as the value systems that are being played out. In gossip conversations we are thinking out loud in order to process how we feel about certain situations. However, we are not dealing with our internal world or our personal value system.

7. *Communing Conversations*

Communing Conversations are we-centered exchanges that are all about sharing information, listening to, being listened to by the other. These conversations are treasured gifts because they are all about genuine connection. When a marriage or a relationship is askew, the first thing that a lot of psychologists do is teach the couple how to communicate using this communing perspective.

Communing conversations engage your inner soul-centered world to create community, not illusions. In these conversations you are *talking to* another person and sharing your life. These conversations have depth and are all about making meaning with another in your life—a two-way street. They are heart-centered and we-centered forms of communication. Communing conversations create meaning and higher states of consciousness in all of us and inspire us to live in the Healthy Side of life—they move us forward toward meaning and purpose.

CHAPTER 10

THE SPECTRUM OF CHANGE IN SOUL TRANSFORMATION

The spectrum of change and movement toward soul transformation happens everyday in some small or monumental way. It can be unexpected, expected as in a natural life span transition, or be a personal choice where you consciously change the direction and focus of your life. The spectrum encompasses everything from the devastatingly negative, to the perfectly positive, all the way to the Divine. It comes in many forms: from disasters, terrorist attacks, revolutions, earthquakes, deaths, accidents, curve balls, traumas, illness, meeting your soul-mate, marriage, getting a new job, or a numinous, miraculous, or spiritual experience. Any of these situations can affect your internal world and have an impact on your psychological and spiritual development. They may even have the capacity to deepen your relationship to your Invisible Actor and the Divine Side of your life.

Smaller changes are easier to work through, whether they be an inner or outer world experience, but no one is ever prepared for the intensity and unpredictability of dramatic changes, even though they are an intrinsic part of human life. Perhaps we all get caught in an illusion that life is automatically going to go into the direction that we want it to? Or, maybe we like being in the illusion of immortality? Reality, especially when it comes to change and soul transformation, is always difficult to face unless it is a personal choice, and then it still may not be easy. It is my perspective that when we are at the intense edges of the polarities of change, we have the capacity to soar into soul transformation—that is, if we dare.

Since I have already discussed inner world soul transformational experiences with the numinous, miraculous, and the spiritual, here I will mostly focus on outer world changes that exist along the spectrum because they are part of the environmental contextual factors that affect us. Unexpected change instantaneously breaks illusions and shatters the world around us. These unexpected, unthinkable situations have a quality of *unknown uncertainty*. The *Who I am!* and *Who I thought I was!* don't seem to match at this time. The greater the intensity of the change, the more significant the chaos will be in your inner world. Monumental unexpected changes include everything from Japan's 2011 quake tsunami nuclear crisis, Egypt's 2/11 revolution, 2010 Haiti earthquake, 2008 market crash, 2004 tsunami, New York's 9/11, Madrid's 3/11, to the untimely deaths of major political figures such as John F. Kennedy, Martin Luther King Jr., and Robert Kennedy or artists such as Michael Jackson and Elvis Presley. These unpredictable events have affected us and to some degree have thrown us into a state of chaos because of the human, animal, and environmental tragedies—it is the unthinkable becoming thinkable. One of the consequences of unexpected change, whether it be big or small, is that there is an opportunity to rework your inner structure and perhaps become a healthier individual. However, not everyone takes this opportunity: instead many people perpetuate negative ways to approach change.

Negative approaches to change are everywhere, but here I want to bring your attention to three of the most common ones. These three roles have previously been addressed in the Shadow Side of The Trinity Model and include the Victim, the Narcissist, and the Disassociate. The Victim role deals with the *poor me* and *why did this happen to me* aspect of change. This approach is all about self-blame, which subsequently creates a sinking, depressive state in an individual. The second is to take the role of a Narcissistic, a me-centered approach, where you go into a state of anger and denial about the situation. Individuals using this approach would ask questions or make statements like *I can't believe that this happened to me*? and, *I do not deserve this kind of punishment!* They see change as a personal attack rather than a life process. The third approach is to take the role of the Disassociate, the energy of the Escape Artist, which is one of denial and not attending to the reality of the situation. To disassociate is to escape your reality into another one, transferring one illusion to another illusion. Even though I separate these three approaches as the main ones, there are many others that may prevent you from partaking in the soul transformational component of any life-altering experience, event, or situation.

When we are in the middle of enormous change, it can be devastating, tragic, and chaotic, and these emotions may require some time to process before we can embrace the gifts of soul transformation that change can bring. Some people involved in disastrous situations, however, may be enlivened by the events and find a sense of long-lasting purpose. One example that comes to mind is that of J.R. Martinez whose story was presented to America during the 2011 season of *Dancing with the Stars*. Martinez entered the Army in 2002 and was later deployed to Iraq. Two months into his deployment, his Humvee struck a landmine and he suffered burns covering forty percent of his body, including his face and head. After going through many surgeries and recoveries, he decided to become a motivational speaker. He later landed an acting job on *All My Children* followed by a season on *Dancing with the Stars* 2011, where he won the coveted mirror ball trophy, along with the hearts of people worldwide. His depth of character, artistry, and dancing were breathtakingly soulful. His tragedy and transformation were now opening doors that he had never even imagined possible. The story for each individual or situation is unique, because of the manner in which one handles change, as it is intimately connected to one's past life experiences and soul-centered nature.

When people go through unexpected change, their worst fears manifest, and they are pushed into a process of suffering. Suffering brings with it the ability to see life's illusions. That is why, as painful as suffering is, the positive aspect is that it assists in burning off some of the narcissistic me-centered illusions that have been engraved in your psyche. This burning off of illusions allows for greater flexibility so that you can shift out of old ways of being into new ways of existence. We must also be aware of changing our viewpoint beyond the illusions that we have to face. It is important to know that joy and love do not cut through the illusions that exist in life. It is only through the path of suffering that we have the ability to fully see our illusions and to engage in psychological growth and soul transformation if we choose to do so.

Depending on the intensity of the unexpected situations you encounter, your inner and outer worlds may have collapsed, chaos revealing itself heretofore unrecognized perspectives embedded within your psyche. You feel like you have been transported to another world that seems lawless and nothing feels real except fear of the unknown. In intense situations, the sense of who you thought you were before this unexpected change occurred has now exploded into fragments, perhaps leaving you alone, abandoned, and in despair. For a moment your software operating system seems to have all but disappeared, and at least for a short while, perhaps you are aware of the Invisible Actor within. Soul stirrings and engagements can occur at this time, but you also might have to wrestle with your default position, which is usually that of your contextual factors. The real question to ask yourself is: *Who am I when most of the illusions of my life have gone?* If you loose your home, property, or family, to a tragedy like an earthquake, tsunami, or hurricane, you will probably have to face the question, *Who am I really when my inner and outer world is in chaos?* The old illusion is gone and the new hasn't formed yet.

Unexpected change also occurs more often in our personal lives which can include anything from a traumatic event to a curve ball. Traumatic events would include the untimely death of a child, a tragic car accident where you become paraplegic, being fired after working for a company for twenty-five years, or finding out at sixty-four that your husband gambled away your entire retirement. In contrast, curve balls are less intense situations which could include being diagnosed with hypoglycemia, finding out your boyfriend of two months is actively bisexual, or being given a demotion at work.

I would like you to be open to the possibility that all these unexpected changes in your inner and outer world are actually divine acts that have a purpose of moving you to attain higher states of consciousness. They come into your life to shake up your inner world and promote degrees of psychological growth and soul transformation that redirect you back onto the path toward your salvation. I will present numerous examples from a personal and a collective perspective.

In my late-thirties I was sitting in a parked car at the bottom of a hill of a Hollywood nightclub parking lot waiting for my husband to pay the valet so that we could go home after having a wonderful evening. A woman driving a large four-wheel drive crashed into me. Needless to say, I had not yet put my seat belt on and was badly hurt. For the next six months I diligently went to physical therapy and acupuncture treatments to reclaim my body. While I was trying to get well on a physical level, something internal was stirring. After six months of intense treatment my body improved and I made a decision to change my life but I didn't know how to get where I wanted to go. The car accident had shifted my psychological state, stirred my soul, and pushed me into psychotherapy. With the guidance of a brilliant Jungian analyst I moved from being an actress to a student enrolling in a masters program in clinical psychology. Before the accident I'd had no intent, inclination, or concept of going back to school. Clearly the accident jolted me into change, and the constrictions that had held my old life together loosened, allowing for realignment with my soul journey. In retrospect, going back to school was the best thing that I could have done, and there is no question that I attained a higher level of consciousness from that experience.

I imagine unexpected changes to be thunderbolts of transformational energy—an immediate movement of being in form to being out of form that can occur on multiple levels simultaneously. For example, if you live in a beautiful home and the next day an electrical fire demolishes it, the form of your home and life automatically changes. Unexpected changes are definitely shocks to our internal structure because they break our psychological pattern, sometimes creating chaos within, which in turn awakens us to the Invisible Actor. Chaos and trauma, though uncomfortable, nourish the soul by shaking loose its constrictions and rigid structures. Chaos allows us to connect with our soul more directly, making the Invisible Actor very present and alert to the new life situation. Breaking through creates space for the Invisible Actor to enliven us, which is why people feel more present and authentic during times of profound change.

Soul engagements and stirrings can be both a personal experience or a collective experience of a country (political and environmental) as seen in Egypt and Tunisia in 2011. During the eighteen-day 2011 Egyptian Revolution, I was glued to CNN watching the daily chaotic events as they occurred. Christians and Muslims, rich and poor joined hands to overthrow the autocratic regime of Hosni Mubarak who had crushed and oppressed his people for thirty years. It was amazing to observe the collective soul of this ancient country at the forefront of this revolution. The people of Egypt had a clear intention, and message along with a determined voice, and in what seemed like an instant, the wall of fear and oppression was dismantled. Their heroic engagement removed the oppressive dictatorship—the heroes were the people standing up for their rights and eventually defeating their appalling regimes. Not only did they reclaim their own souls but also the soul of their nation from the corruption and greed that prevailed. The shackles that constrained them were broken, leaving an entire nation to be reborn in a new form as environmental, political, and governmental contextual factors crashed. It was extraordinary to hear their voices of jubilation as the Egyptian people dropped to their knees, praying and cheering, many in disbelief at the power of their collective voices in the creation of this colossal, unexpected but yearned for change. Many Egyptians painted the colors of their flag on their faces to demonstrate unity and to symbolize their deep devotion to their country. Tears rolled down my eyes as I watched the people participating in Tehrir Square engaging the Hero within—willing to die in order for their country to live. Inspired by the spark and interconnection of social media networks, these people joined hands, some bloodied, to take back their dignity through the power of nonviolence. The Egyptian people were empowered individually as well as collectively: Their own souls were enlivened along with the soul of the country. Egypt and its people will never be the same because of that awe-inspiring day on which Egyptian destiny moved the arc of history toward justice for the first time in thirty years.

Also deeply etched in my memory is New York's 9/11 when the shock and horror of what happened to the Twin Towers were still very present in America's psyche. It felt like our collective humanity was acutely compassionate and more enlivened than it had previously been or even is now. At least for a short while, all Americans, and perhaps people all over the world who were appalled at the events of that tragic day, were more present on a soul level, and I remember feeling a sense of connection to my fellow Americans and to people all over the world that I had not previously felt. Tragedy welcomes community—it is human nature.

When the 2008 market crash revealed itself, it proved that neither financial success nor high intellectual capacity has anything to do with an individual's skill set for change. Even though I am always surprised by how people view economic disasters, I was dumbfounded when I heard about all the billionaires who jumped out of their windows to their death—to them being *millionaires* was unthinkable. For these men, their perception of who they thought they were was narrowly defined by their malfunctioning relationship to money. These unhealthy behaviors and patterns from the Shadow Side were dormant within these men until they made their presence known by taking their tragic leap to the other side of existence.

Ashley's Story

Ashley, a forty-five-year-old court reporter came into treatment because of depression, anxiety, and insomnia issues that were directly related to her carpal tunnel syndrome. She could no longer do the level of computer work that was required of her and as part of the treatment we discussed possible career options. She eventually decided to go back to school to study law. She reached for a higher state of consciousness (other than a victim role) by creating a forward movement to a professional career at the age of forty-two, a life-altering and soul-stirring situation that totally changed her vision of who she thought she was and what was possible. The unexpected result of her curve ball was a forward movement toward a new form of healthy behavior on the Healthy Side of life.

Brad's Story

In another example, Brad, a handsome, dark-haired thirty-three-year-old man came in for a consultation regarding a series of dreams that he'd had. During the intake he told me that he was studying at a university in New Orleans when Hurricane Katrina hit, and though it was a terrible tragedy, he felt transformed by the experience, saying that it was the best thing that ever happened to him because he felt so alive. After things in New Orleans settled down, Brad continued his studies and dedicated as much time as he could to helping families recover from the shock and devastation. He also decided to change his major from business to that of psychology. I could feel his eternal flame quicken as he described his work and experiences with the people of New Orleans. His deep intrinsic desire to help people heal their lives recalibrated after this tragedy. A young man was going in one direction, then in response to the disaster is now going in another direction, one that is authentic and soul-centered. This disaster allowed him to attain a higher level of consciousness by engaging the Invisible Actor within and was subsequently enlivened and sustained by his soul-centered choice.

Different Types of Unexpected Change

Unexpected change and transformation comes in many forms. I was at a seminar when I heard this extraordinary emergency room physician speaking about his work in a Chicago-based hospital located close to violent gang areas. I remember asking him why he chose to practice medicine with that particular population, and he replied that he loved working in the emergency room because he found the people there to be more present emotionally, and therefore more real, because they were dealing with the life and death issues of stabbings and gunshot wounds. As he spoke of his work his eternal flame quickened—the authenticity of the human experience inspired him to work in those very specific and challenging conditions. This doctor, in his own amazing soul-centered way, transformed the lives of the people in the community where he was working.

Unexpected and unthinkable changes are inevitable, sooner or later, in our lives, and we have to be in a perpetual state of readiness. The other day while watching CNN, I heard a news story on *sun storms*. These storms could completely upset the power girds and electronic systems, which could affect all satellite communications, including our cell phones, Internet, radio and television stations, having serious consequences for us all. Adding to this potential disaster are the 2012 predictions that loom in our conscious and unconscious minds. A line from *Star Trek: The Next Generation* comes to mind: "Resistance is futile!" And believe it or not, that's good news.

Life-altering events involving change and transformation whether big or small, positive or negative, have the potential to deepen our connection to body and soul. They shake up and shatter our world and any illusions that we had about our situation. An example of a positive life-altering experience comes to mind. During the 2009 auditions of "Britain's Got Talent," an unconventional and unlikely contestant, Susan Boyle, captured the hearts and imagination of the world with her *bravura* singing performance of *I Dreamed a Dream*. Even though she did not win the contest, she *"went viral"* on YouTube, and the success of her first album was unprecedented. However, right after the contest, Ms. Boyle had to check into a psychiatric hospital to deal with her erratic behavior and anxiety. Clearly, the shift from small-town Scottish recluse to global singing sensation brought chaos to her outer life which in turn agitated her formerly modulated inner life. We can't possibly know the ultimate outcome for Ms. Boyle, but we can marvel at her life journey.

Expected or Chosen Change

In contrast to unexpected changes, when we expect change or choose change we create a conscious and calculated forward-focused momentum. Expected changes are usually associated with natural lifespan transitions such as college, marriage, having a baby, midlife upheavals, and retiring. Even though we choose some of these transitions, but we might not choose all the changes that accompany them. When we choose change like retooling, going back to school, moving to a new geographic or even choosing to participate in spiritual or miraculous experiences we may not be prepared for all that occurs either. Either way the intensity of change on which you are embarking may take a lot of conscious maneuvering because your inner psychological state will likely put you into a sea of chaos whether you want it or not. Choosing change in your life can come in many forms: leaving a marriage that you are miserable in, even though you may have to give half of your wealth to your wife, leaving your stable but soul-crushing office job for a creative soul-enriching job that pays half of the salary; moving from an extravagant home to one that is simple and affordable; or moving to another city or area that is far away from your family and contextual factors to find yourself; going on a three-month mediation retreat to free yourself from attachments; traveling to India to study with some enlightened masters; studying world religions; going back to school to get a PhD; or going to a psychologist to help save your marriage. I think of how many marriages could have been transformed, including my own, if a partner had had the ability to do the unthinkable—to go to therapy. But there are individuals who don't want to change, or are too afraid to change, and instead play their dysfunctional contextual factors and story like a broken record over and over. Fear holds them back and they remain in a gridlocked pattern. Unfortunately, in the end, everyone loses because of their unhealthy contextual factors. However, even when you choose change, you go through the process of collapsing your inner and outer structures—there is no other way for change to occur. *Change is about surrendering to a new way of being.*

The Soul Transformation Process

The *soul transformation process* is another perspective through which to experience change, whether that change is unexpected or expected. This five-phase process is all about shifting stances, so that you can re-create and re-energize your life. The phases include detaching yourself from the events of the situation; connecting to the four Divine Truths; creating a new positive feeling stance answering four questions; creating a stance of compassion and forgiveness; and then moving about the world with this new positive stance.

The soul transformation process is all about enlivening your willingness to live in a positive mode, the mode of soul. This may not be the easiest thing to do when you have just experienced unexpected pain, trauma, or curveballs, but all I can say is that it can really help you shift your focus and take responsibility, which automatically re-empowers you. Engaging the soul transformation process requires that you go into a deep, silent space and align with the four Divine Truths that are based in Eastern philosophy: eternal peace, eternal truth, eternal love, and right moral and ethical judgment and action. I present two examples of the soul transformation process from a personal and professional perspective and a guided soul transformation process at the end of this section. Taken together, the examples and the guided soul transformation process can deepen your understanding of the soul transformation process.

If you unexpectedly caught your boyfriend having an affair with another woman, for example, you would initially feel hurt, angry, and betrayed. If you stayed in this unhealthy emotional stance and perpetuated it by ruminating on your grievances, you would go deeper into the illusion of the Shadow Side and perhaps engage one of the default positions of the Victim, Narcissist, or Disassociate. This is not to say that you shouldn't be angry and enraged at your boyfriend's behavior—you should, at least for little while . . . *and then you must move on.* When you are ready to move on, you must detach yourself from the story or situation and take responsibility for your role in it and *own* that you made a choice to be in that relationship. Opening up yourself to this new frame of reference helps you to make a choice about how long you want to stay in an unhealthy emotional stance. If you look at this situation from the perspective of your boyfriend's character, you would not wish to align, or be in relationship, with this type of man. In fact, you would be glad that he is not a part of your life. In the long run it would be better for you to face the illusions about your boyfriend prior to marriage rather than after you were married. This process also requires that you recognize that your boyfriend also made a choice, and the choice was not about you. He showed a lack of boundaries, a lack of respect, and a lack of integrity in response to the relationship that you had with him. Clearly, you would not want to partner with a man who is capable of this type of behavior if you want to live a happy life. So now it is time to *detach yourself* from the events of the situation—the who, what, when, where, and how of the illusions in which you were caught, the first phase.

In the second phase you must engage the four Divine Truths by silently communing with your Invisible Actor. These are discussed in depth in the Guided Soul Transformation Process section. In the third phase you need to conjure a different image and frame of reference, coming from a feeling perspective of what you would want for yourself in regard to a healthy relationship, focusing on the present and future rather than on your past. At this time you need to answer four specific questions:

- How do I want to feel in regard to this story or situation?

- What are the four qualities with which I want to align?

- What do I feel about how others treat me when I embody this new stance?

- How do I feel when I meet someone professionally or personally who embodies those same qualities?

The answers to these questions are powerful because if you want to be in a healthy relationship with those qualities, then you must *have* those qualities yourself. Let's say you choose *loyalty, integrity, honesty,* and *respect.* You need to imagine how you yourself would personally feel if you had these qualities at this time. Go into a relaxed silent space and connect with each of these four qualities, and, one at a time, *breathe* them into your body. When you complete this integration, then imagine how you would feel if you were with a man who respected these qualities in you and had the same qualities himself. Remember, *your inner world creates your outer world.* This positive stance will make you feel beautiful, uplifted, and radiant. Rehearse these feeling stances over and over until you feel your soul transforming.

In the fourth phase you need to shift your stance again and look at your cheating boyfriend (or whomever has hurt, betrayed, or offended you) from the perspective of compassion and forgiveness rather than hatred, because you now choose to remain in the highest of integrity and not lower your standards to the Shadow Side. This entire process takes time, sometimes months. In the Soul Transformation Process you are shifting your stance and perspective from despair and rage to eternal peace, eternal truth, eternal love, and right moral and ethical judgment and action. In the process you are taking a higher emotional stance: *the high road.* When you come from this perspective you stay out of the wounds of the experience, and you are able to take greater control of your own life and destiny. A very wise spiritual teacher once told me that the way in which you end one relationship is how you begin a new relationship. Since that time I have always followed this perspective and taught it to my patients. So stay in the

Healthy Side of this experience, have compassion and forgiveness for your boyfriend, and move forward in your new life with grace and dignity. You will feel clear and clean with your right action and be available emotionally for your next relationship. Your boyfriend will, however, have to live with his choice and carry his Shadow Side baggage with him because none of us can ever take back what we have already done. He can choose to psychologically repair what he has done, but in essence: What's done is done!

In the fifth phase you move into the world with this new stance. You "walk your talk." You take your freshly minted state of being into the world, into your personal, social, and work relationships. This soul-infused stance will automatically transform your life.

In another example let's say that you lost your job because of the economy, which in turn makes you feel very angry and resentful. If you stayed in that angry and resentful negative stance, you would engage the Shadow Side and go deeper into the illusion of yourself as victim. In the first phase you first must detach yourself from the event of loosing your job from the who, what, when, where, and how of the illusions in which you were caught. Then in the second phase commune with your Invisible Actor in a silent relaxed space and go into a deep meditative stance to align with the four Divine Truths: eternal peace, eternal truth, eternal love, and right moral and ethical judgment and action. Take responsibility for being in that job, knowing that there was a potential for getting laid off or being fired, and that you did nothing about it but continued working because you needed to pay your mortgage and support your family. Taking responsibility allows you to open up to a new frame of reference that can shift your victim stance and re-empower you.

Now in this third phase you need to conjure up a different image, a different picture of your life, focusing on your present and future and how you would want to feel when you have a great job, one at which you are successful and respected for your talent. You need to answer the same four questions from our previous example that will help you choose how you want to deal with the situation:

- How do I want to feel in regard to this story or situation?

- What are the four qualities with which I want to align?

- What do I feel about how others treat me when I embody this new stance?

- How do I feel when I meet someone professionally or personally who embodies those same qualities?

Answer each question. Remember the importance of the four qualities that you would like to have when you are working in that professional situation. If you want to be in a work situation that values those qualities, you must also have those qualities within yourself. Let's say you choose *respect, trustworthiness, professionalism,* and *dedication* as your four qualities. Then imagine yourself working for an employer who both values those qualities in you and also has them in him or herself. Rehearse those positive feeling stances over and over until you feel your soul transforming.

In the fourth phase, shift your stance back to the company that laid you off and have compassion and forgiveness for that choice. Breathe compassion and forgiveness into your body, letting go of any negativity. When you remove yourself from the wounds of the situation, you will have more control over your life. Moreover, in the final phase you will be sending out your resumes with a very different energy and perspective than you would have if you had if you sent them out prior to this process. Take a moment to enjoy the grace and co-creation of your new life and work.

Guided Soul Transformation Process

Phase One: Detach Yourself from the Events of the Situation

Go into a silent relaxed space and detach yourself from the, who, what, when, where, and how of the situation, event, or experience in which you are caught. Sit or lie down and be in silence. Breathe deeply, following each breath. Imagine your story as a movie in which you are acting. Do not attach to the story, just experience it from the perspective of a silent, neutral observer. This process is incredibly hard to do, but it is essential to separate yourself from the wounds of the situation because the events of the story can give rise to illusions that do not reflect the truth about you.

If you are having difficulty because you are still reacting emotionally to your story, then you look at the emotions as sensations of the body. View these body sensations as neutral descriptions such as *darkness, lightness, heaviness, tingly, dull, throbbing, full, slow, fast, full* or *empty,* to name a few. When using this perspective do not refer to the wounds as emotions, just as *sensations,* because doing so will help you to detach.

The story is something that has happened to you, a life experience, but it is not who you essentially are. You must take the emotional charge out of the situation so that you can move forward with this soul transformation process. Every time a thought breaks through into consciousness, make a choice to *not* engage it, but just see it as a mini-movie floating by, and go back to following your breath.

Besides detaching from the story, you must also take responsibility for being in that story or situation. *Taking responsibility is a crucial step in this process!* Remember, you are not the story, event, situation, or experience. It is necessary to complete this detachment process before you go to the next phase. You will know when you are ready to move forward when you can go through this phase, in its entirety, without any disturbing emotion.

Phase Two: Connect to the Four Divine Truths

From a silent, relaxed place, follow your breath, noticing the ebb and flow of your physical body. Do not attach to any thoughts that break through, just continue visualizing them as mini-movies that you do not wish to engage with, because you are consciously choosing to follow your breath. When you are in *silence and in a state of inner peace,* focus on bringing the Divine Truths, one at a time, into your body.

First recall a memory that is associated with one of the Divine Truths. For example, when I think of eternal peace, I remember a time when I was by myself, very calm and peaceful, lying on the sand of a deserted beach just hearing the waves as they ebbed and flowed. Once you have identified the memory associated with the Divine Truth, bring the Divine Truth up the spine on the *in-breath*, and on the *out-breath* release the Divine Truth down the front of the body and then circulate it.

Begin with *eternal peace*. Recall a memory or moment when you felt very peaceful and hold this memory in mind as you breathe in *eternal peace*. Stay connected to this process until you feel the energy of eternal peace circulating throughout your body.

Next breathe in *eternal truth,* following that same pathway. Recall a memory when you felt the clarity of truthfulness and hold that in your mind as you breathe the words *eternal truth,* following the same breath pathway.

Now do the same for *eternal love*, remembering a time when you felt unconditionally loved by someone or a time when you loved someone unconditionally, and breathe that memory/sensation/feeling in the same way.

Finally, in order to connect to *right moral and ethical judgment and action*, remember a time when you did the right thing and were in the highest level of your integrity. Locate that memory in your body as you breathe in right moral and ethical judgment and action, using that same breath pathway.

You may need to preplan these four memories to make the process easier. If you can't find a personal memory, use literature, history, or cinema sources as examples. Spend a couple of minutes in silence enjoying the four Divine Truths circulating and enlivening the Invisible Actor within. Do not continue with the next phase until you feel comfortable with your progress in this phase.

Phase Three: Create a New Positive Feeling Stance Answering the Four Questions

From a silent, relaxed space ask yourself the four questions on at a time:

- How do I want to feel in regard to this story or situation?

- What are the four qualities with which I want to align?

- What do I feel about how others treat me when I embody this new stance?

- How do I feel when I meet someone professionally or personally who embodies those same qualities?

Begin with the first question: *How do I want to feel in regard to this story or situation?* Answer this question focusing on the present and future simultaneously.

Then ask yourself the second question: *What are the four qualities with which I want to align?* Knowing the four positive emotional qualities, whether they are personal or professionally based, will give you a different viewpoint of the story or situation and help you to further detach from it. Immerse yourself in the feeling state of each quality, one at a time, and continue following your breath, moving up your spine and down the front of your body, then circulating the energy throughout your body, not attaching to any static in your mind.

Now ask yourself the third question: *What do I feel about how others treat me when I embody this new stance?* When you have answered this question and feel complete with this process, breathe that stance into your body, using that same pathway. Now move on to question four: *How do I feel when I meet someone, professionally or personally, who embodies those same qualities?* Now experience this new state as you breathe it throughout your body, enjoying each of these new feeling stances. Stay in this sacred space for a couple of minutes, or as long as you like, until you feel complete and then proceed to the fourth phase.

Phase Four: Create a Stance of Compassion and Forgiveness

From a silent, relaxed space, create a stance of compassion and forgiveness for the situation that occurred or the person who caused you harm or hurt. This may be difficult, but you must let go of the wounding. Circulate these two qualities of compassion and forgiveness, one at a time, up your spine, down the front, and then expanding them throughout your body. This stage is vitally important because it helps to remove the negative energy of the experience from your body, making room for a new stance, a new way of being, to be born into your life. Continue this process until you feel good about yourself. When you have completed this process, *own* that you are in a place of compassion and forgiveness and hold this position for a couple of minutes. When you feel complete with this process move on to the final phase.

Phase Five: Move about in the World with This New Positive Stance

Know that you are making a conscious choice to participate in the Divine and Healthy Sides of life as you move about the world with your new positive stance. Know that you are infused with the four Divine Truths, the four preferred qualities, as well as with forgiveness and compassion for the situation—it is the Soul Transformation Process completed. It may take you some time to really complete all the phases. It took me a couple of months to fully shift a situation on which I was working, so take your time because the results are worth it.

Shame

Shame is an emotional response that surfaces when you are going through varying degrees of change. Facing shame is difficult because it exposes Shadow Side material that change and transformation have exposed. Shame can feel constricting because of its engrained me-centered aspects and contextual factors that are etched in your psyche. It is important to understand that shame lies beneath the processes of change on any level, so you need to make it your ally. Cleaning up your alignment with shame opens up the space for change and soul transformation. By *shame* I mean your personal evaluation of situations or events from your past in which you felt embarrassed, disgraced, humiliated, or inadequate. To admit shame can be a painful process, even though doing so actually brings the relief of a spoken truth: "I feel ashamed." It is very unfortunate that we all have such a difficult time expressing shame because it is a valuable emotion with which every person on the planet has to deal. Perhaps shame is illuminated when the goals or ideas that you have for your life don't manifest like you wanted. If you do not deal with your shame, the default position may be a cowardice stance along with many other emotions located in the Shadow Side. Do you want that? When you are undergoing change or are in any type of soul transformation process, you must choose the direction of your life wisely.

Underneath shame lie two Shadow Side qualities: low self-esteem and low self-confidence. Low self-esteem depletes all your emotional expressions, including joy and delight, and low self-confidence impairs your level of judgment, and your personal capacities. These negative qualities develop over time and may spawn self-sabotaging and unhealthy behaviors, patterns and roles located in the Shadow Side such as the saboteur.

Getting through shame requires a lot of courage. Courage does not come naturally to everyone. Most of us need coaches to cheer us forward. Just think of the Olympic athlete who emerged from small-town America to win a gold metal. Besides physical ability, mental acuity, and spiritual capacity, he or she was able to change and achieve success because of a coach who was teacher, mentor, and stabilizing force in his or her life. All athletes at this Olympic level have a coach, because without these skilled professionals most of these athletes would have not have changed sufficiently to achieve their levels of excellence or international success. One of the many qualities that these coaches teach and foster is courage—the courage to keep trying and the courage to change perceptions and visions of what the athlete believes is possible. If you can't change or move out of your unhealthy behaviors and patterns of shame, maybe you need a courage coach, mentor, or psychologist to help you move your life forward. Some families have the ability to provide all the courage coaching that you may need: however, not all families have that ability.

Having a great support system is essential for a healthy life, especially when you are going through change. Friends, colleagues, and next-door neighbors can make great support systems. Families can also provide this role if they are healthy, but sometimes that might not even be enough. Find a way to give yourself the support that you need.

Life *is* Change

Life is about continuous change. Change increases our consciousness level and our quality of life if we allow it. As I have previously stated, many of us generally hate change and transformation because we fear the unknown and this fear keeps us from moving forward. I want to inspire you to think of change as an adventure, a movement toward a new consciousness. Befriend change. I want you to imagine it as if you were traveling to a new country where you learned new things and had amazing experiences. When new information comes into your world, allow it to change you in some way. You have within your inner world a plethora of "countries" to explore along with your Invisible Actor to take you to deeper soul experiences. The benefit is that you don't have to take a plane or spend any money on this adventure—it is *inner world traveling*. Whether you are working psychologically or using a soul transformation approach, you will move to a different place and a different consciousness level. Nature provides us with a perfect example: a caterpillar becomes a butterfly, and when the butterfly takes its maiden flight, there is no remnant of the caterpillar. The inner and outer worlds of the caterpillar have completely transformed. All you see is the butterfly soaring into the vast blue sky. Do some inner-world traveling, engage your Invisible Actor, and open your eyes to the divinity that exists in the world within you and soar into new life dimensions.

CHAPTER 11

THE COMPENSATION FACTOR

C haracter development is a complex process. Compensation is an aspect of character development and a natural part of the growth process that we all do consciously or unconsciously. Between the ages three to six there is a compensatory habitual coping mechanism that instinctively develops which I term *the compensation factor*. It occurs in response to an intense experience or a progression of experiences on the Healthy, Shadow, or Divine Sides of life. It is extraordinarily important because it affects how you conduct your life. The compensation factor can be positive or negative and include anything from winning an award, saving an animal, having a numinous experience, to traumatic experiences such as, moving, death, divorce, and being orphaned, to name a few. Actually any type of experience, big or even small, can create a reaction and compensation to a real-life situation.

A historical example of the compensation factor is evident in the extraordinary, mythical and mysterious life of Eva Perone. Eva was born in a small village two hundred miles from Buenos Aries, the fifth and youngest illegitimate child of Juana, a peasant woman, and Juan, a small rancher. As the story has been told, when Eva was one-year-old her father abandoned the family and moved back with his first family, leaving Juana to fend for all the five children alone. Through their formative years the children had to endure the intense shame of their illegitimacy and were often shunned by other children and adults living in the community. When Eva was six-years-old her father died. She and her siblings wanted to attend his funeral, but because they were considered illegitimate, they were only allowed to trail the mourners. This public rejection and humiliation deeply affected Eva and she swore that she would never be in the position of being last again—*being first*—became her compensation factor. Eva remained true to her internal commitment and made her way to Buenos Aires at the tender age of fifteen. From that time onward she began her meteoric rise to become the most famous First Lady of Argentina, propelled by the determination of her compensation factor. It is my understanding that we all have at least one of these compensation traits, in which we engage throughout our lifespan, and of which we are unconscious until we bring consciousness to it.

Your compensation factor is a way that you move about in the world. It is a stance that you unconsciously created and selected from a pattern of behavior that had already been etched within your character structure because of your contextual factors. It may have emerged because of survival instincts; it is your gut instinct emerging into form as a reaction to a situation. This gut reaction may or may not be a winning strategy however, bringing consciousness to this coping mechanism is paramount for growth because it can start taking over your life, and you may not even be conscious about it.

Your compensation factor emerges from within your character structure and is part of your hard drive. Since you can't change it, all you can do is to bring consciousness to it because it is a stance that organically emerged as a reaction to an event or situation, that over time, became a part of your personality structure. This unconscious creation has both positive and negative ramifications. I will provide you numerous examples.

José's Story

José was a good-looking Latino male in his late thirties when I met him. His parents had brought the family from Guatemala to the United States to find a new life when he was just three, but unfortunately establishing a new life, in a new culture, was not as easy as they thought. There were green card issues, financial issues, and relational issues. The pressure of all these problematic areas combined with raising three children, were more than José's parents could handle. Fighting, lying, drinking and infidelity soon became the parental mode of behavior.

José, the middle boy, desperately needed attention and parenting, but he didn't get much. As an alternative he tried to find multiple ways to escape from the insanity of his household; he tried sports, and he even helped with the chores around the house to make it easier for his mom. However, neither of these suited his sensitive nature or took care of his needs. He also tried reading, but boys who read were deemed sissy. He needed to find a way to push away from all the anguish and despair he was feeling. He eventually found his way to escape the insanity and went into the role of the Disassociate and became an *Escape Artist*, a stance created in his childhood that was fully engaged by his Shadow Side by the time he was sixteen—solace in the bottle.

The parental fighting escalated and when Jose was seventeen, his father hung himself. José's drinking continued, more feverishly than before. After his father's funeral, his mother moved back to Guatemala, leaving him with his eighteen-year-old bother. His brother married three months after his mother's departure, which left José to fend for himself, alone. At eighteen, José joined the military, making Desert Storm his destination. The military was good for him because it gave him some structure, but it also allowed for an even deeper pattern of escaping from reality to emerge—moving all over the world. After completing his military service, José was unable to put down any roots for longer than two years. He just kept on moving: Ohio, Texas, Indiana, Guatemala, Germany, and California. Escaping from his internal and external reality became the driving force that shaped his life—it was his compensation factor. José got sober at thirty-six, was now thirty-eight, in AA, working the Twelve Step Program, and slowly bringing consciousness to the Escape Artist that lived within.

When you are engaged in the depth of this pattern of compensation as the Escape Artist, you are not able to engage your authentic self because it is a though you are sleepwalking. In José's case his compensation factor was an organic reaction to an abusive life situation that was about self-protection and survival. Because he had a hard time staying grounded, we worked with meditation and spiritual practices to keep him calm and centered. These techniques assisted him in bringing a deeper level of consciousness to his unhealthy patterns, and moving him toward being present in the *here and now*, which lay the foundation for him to connect with his Invisible Actor. When José finally connects with his Invisible Actor, his life will transform, and he will be on his authentic soul journey.

Ted's Story

Ted was a big, burly, good-looking guy in his thirties. Growing up, his father was always on the road, thereby physically and emotionally unavailable to him. His mother, on the other hand, was always available, with an emotional style of critical perfectionism, demanding it from everyone around her. Ted, their only child, eventually developed a clumsy stance to compensate for his mother's addiction to perfection. He knew he could never be like her, nor did he want to be. Being clumsy brought him some positive reactions, from his mother as well as from others, especially girls. He could now get the attention he desperately needed by being clumsy, and adorable, which eventually got him the nickname of *Teddy Bear*. Being clumsy was an unconscious compensation reaction to his mother's perfectionism. This clumsy stance became very popular with women who had a strong nurturing tendency, and he got a lot of dates because of it. So why should he change it? But the question is, who really is Ted, when he is not in his compensation reaction? When asked, he did not know!

Do you know what your compensation factor is? How do you use it in life? How would knowing your compensation factor change the way you think about your life? Answering these questions will give you a deeper glimpse into how you live your life.

My Compensation Factor

My grandmother, though not by blood, came to live with us when I was born to help with the household and caretaking responsibilities because my parents worked. My grandmother became my *Guardian Angel*—I called her *Baba*. I was extremely blessed to have her care for me. Her nature was gentle, sweet, and very loving. There was nothing better than sleeping spoons with her at night—it was like being in Heaven. One of my fondest memories was playing airplanes—we would imagine that we were airplanes, taking off from the kitchen chairs and that had to land quickly on the linoleum floor beneath us. It was so much fun!!!

Unfortunately, good things come to an end. Over time, my mother became enraged by my affectionate relationship with Baba, and the friction in the air thickened. My mother was not warm and fuzzy like my Baba, and given the choice, you know whose arms I would go to. My mother's driving force was money—nothing else mattered which may have been her compensation for being orphaned at the age of two. Nevertheless, I vividly remember the day my life changed. I was about five years old. I was in the basement of our house playing dress-up with my grandmother, having the time of my life. My mother unexpectedly came home, saw us playing, dress-up and went ballistic. Her rage was intolerable and years of pent-up anger exploded into the room as she screamed and yelled at us for playing dress-up and then viciously shamed my grandmother for allowing it. I became undeniably aware of her wrath and power that day. It felt like the day after that situation occurred that my grandmother's bags were packed, and she was moved to a senior citizens home in a town thirty-five miles away. I was devastated at the turn of events. Grief and loss became my new constant companions. I knew I had to become a different person, so I hid that fun-loving child that I had been and became an obedient child in order to survive. I did everything my mother said because I didn't want to deal with her wrath—I was scared of her. She ruled the family with an iron fist and we all had to obey her, including my father. So, at five I survived by being *obedient* and doing everything that she said. It was how I ran my life. I learned how to cook, clean, and excel at every task that I was given. A new life was dawning . . . Heaven was now a fading memory.

By the time I was twelve years old, being obedient was deeply engrained into my psyche. Working at the family business, a dry goods store in Two Hills, was not a problem as I had already learned how to juggle many things at once—slave labor. After school I would work from four to six, Fridays four to nine, and Saturdays all day. On Sundays I would usually have to wash the floor and tidy up the display sections for the following week. During the week it was also my responsibility to make dinner for the family because my mother had to count the money so she could take the deposit to the bank the next day. When my mother would get home, dinner had to be ready on the table for the family, or else. After dinner I washed the dishes, then I could do my homework. I often felt like the first part of the Cinderella story, where the wicked stepmother gives her these unbelievable tasks to do. I would have much rather been in the last part were the prince shows up, but that wasn't my story.

I survived my childhood by being obedient and getting things done. *Obedience* was my compensation factor. With time my obedience moved to proficiency and the ability to handle many things simultaneously. I used the childhood abuse as a discipline to accomplish things and to this day I am driven to accomplish things. I have developed an internal *Task Master* that drives me and enables me to achieve a lot of things in my life, but I also suffer because of it. I can easily become a *Doing Machine*, losing my balance for living a healthy fulfilling life.

In reaction to my mother's drive for money, I became a seeker of heart. It is no surprise that I chose heart-centered creative careers such as acting and psychology, rather than getting a degree in economics or law. Money is certainly something that I like, especially when it comes to designer clothes and shoes, but I am not driven by it. I saw what it did to my family, and I didn't want to end up like them—although I will readily admit that I have a material-spiritual split.

Exploring Your Compensation Factor

Exploring your compensation factor and journaling about it brings another level of consciousness to your life. This process of figuring it out may take a while, so just be patient. I suggest that you begin by writing about ways that you compensated in terms of your birth order, like being the middle child, being the baby of the family, or even being the only child as the first place you begin. Then remember any incidents, events, or geographic moves that happened to you during the ages of three to six. Write about those experiences and see what emerges. If you need assistance and your family members are not helpful, then I suggest you work with a psychologist to assist you in the process. Knowing your compensation factor is really valuable in trying to know yourself.

We can only make changes and adjustments to things when there is a greater freedom of choice, and it is easier to move to different possibilities when we are not caught in shadowland coping mechanisms. Greater emotional balance staying closer to the *center-point* of the pendulum—characterizes healthy individuals. None of us is perfect, and we all struggle to stay on track. By doing your spiritual practice and connecting with your Invisible Actor on a daily basis, you can find peace and balance in your life.

CHAPTER 12

THE SOUL TRANSFORMATION BLUEPRINT

was inspired to create a pathway for discovering our soul purpose and deepening our understanding of self. What emerged was *The Soul Transformation Blueprint,* a template that helps you assess what is important in your life and to identify how you live your life. The Soul Transformation Blueprint helps you express qualities with which you wish to align, integrates your personality characteristics, and addresses questions such as: *Who am I? Where am I in life? Where am I going?* and *What is my soul purpose?* The Soul Transformation Blueprint makes a poignant statement about your life by incorporating aspects of the Invisible Actor along with the Healthy, Shadow, and Divine Sides of life. I will present examples from both aspirational and realistic perspectives.

Your Soul Transformation Blueprint is comprised of seven categories:

1. Your value system.

2. The roles you play.

3. The way you sell yourself to the world.

4. Your brand.

5. Your shadow qualities.

6. Your compensation factor.

7. The desired outcomes of your life.

I provide you with examples as well as a template at the end of the chapter.

The Trinity Model is very helpful in pointing out in which side of life you partake. The Healthy Side qualities enhance the positive aspects of life, which in turn can be transformational for the people with whom you interact—your friends, family, and co-workers. We all know people who are guided by these values. Just think of some of your family members, mentors, and teachers who have helped you to grow. These healthy values and qualities include everything from integrity, congruency, and thoughtfulness, to courage, flexibility, efficiency, sincerity, and friendliness. Individuals using these Healthy Side qualities tend to be enhancement oriented which means that they prefer to nurture, improve, and expand rather than destroy, decline, and contract. However, these people are not exempt from having negative things happen to them like natural disasters, trauma, crisis, pain, and curve balls, but the manner in which they deal with these obstacles is different—they try make their negative situations into positive ones—it is part of their authentic self.

The Shadow Side qualities involve negative values and roles. Individuals who come from this perspective focus on things like never having enough money, never getting lucky, never getting a break, never meeting Mr. Right, never being understood, or no one ever cares about them . . . the list goes on and on. We all know people who approach life from this perspective because they do not want to take responsibility for the ills that befall them. A lot of them like playing the role of the Victim, and the Narcissist, because they can lament their wounds and life's injustices ad infinitum. Other's like to escape, like the Disassociate. There are many more Shadow Side roles that express their unprocessed wounds for everyone to hear or see. When Shadow Side things happen to them, they use it as another validation for how bad their life is, and they try to make you feel sorry for them. These individuals stay stuck in this position because they either do not know how to get out of it, are unconscious of it, or are unable to get out because they are caught in their contextual factors.

Divine Side qualities are incredibly positive as long as they are balanced in reality. Divine qualities include everything from the mystical, sacred, holy, heavenly, blissful, rapturous to the simply spiritual. However like any positive quality, if moved too far down the spectrum, they can shift into the Shadow Side—just think of the incidents at Heavens Gate, Jonestown, and Waco, Texas.

Working Through the Seven Soul Transformation Blueprint Categories

The first category of the Soul Transformation Blueprint is your *value system,* which comprises the ethical and moral foundations for your life. These are the qualities that you aspire to express in your life—integrity, honor, truthfulness, trustworthiness, virtue, morality, decency, fairness, strength, sincerity, and creativity, to name a sampling. You need to meditate and commune with your Invisible Actor to create the best and most authentic moral and ethical judgment and action for yourself. Writing down the process in your journal could really help you make specific choices.

The second category, the *roles that you play* reflect the way that you move about in the world. These roles are connected to both your private and work life and can be expressed on both sides of the spectrum. Examples include creator, originator, empowerer, controller, balancer, producer, collaborator, healer, trailblazer, intellectual, to manipulator, victim, or a me-centered player, to name a few. Even though your spectrum of choice is enormous, each choice must emerge from within your authentic side and realistically embody how you act in the world.

The third category is comprised of the *qualities that you sell to the world*. Sometimes these may be similar to the roles from the second category. By the time we are adults, many of us exhibit qualities that have been fixed within our character structure either by being unconsciously setup prior to birth, created by the roles that we played in our family or were co-created, or shaped by our personal life experiences. These qualities are essentially the ones that we present to the world on a daily basis; they are how we want others to perceive us. You will probably have more than one quality that you will sell, so you should really analyze what you do on a daily basis. What you sell at work may be different than what you sell at home, so include both. This may be harder to figure out so you may have to ask your family, friends, and co-workers for help. Your answers must be clear, honest, and authentic which will give you a deeper understanding of yourself. When one of these selling qualities becomes more prominent than the rest, it may be associated with the brands that you are selling.

The fourth category is your *brand,* and by that I mean an identifiable quality or emotion that is uniquely associated with you. Corporations, celebrities, and sports stars use the concept of branding all the time, so why shouldn't you? Your brand must be authentic because inauthentic brands don't sell. You will also need to be cognizant on which side your brand is—Healthy, Shadow, or Divine Side—because each side has a different market. You should also be aware of the audience you sell your brand to: your children, husband, family, boss, or society at large. Just for fun look around your office and figure out what brand your co-workers are selling—it could be very interesting information. I actually processed this with a colleague at the office where I was working. The office manager's brand was "competency and efficiency" while the other staff members brands included everything from "come and get me," to "sweetness," to "quirky and efficient," to "exuberant deception," to "let me help you so I can line my pockets." The specific intention of any of these choices creates a vastly different outcome, so you need to be very clear. If you don't like your brand because it is in the Shadow Side, then you need to get psychological help to uncover whatever is in the dark.

The fifth category is the ever-present *Shadow Side* with which you need to be acquainted because it can get you into a lot of trouble. It is the part that you don't want to know or don't want anyone else to know. This category is the hardest to face. These dark qualities that comprise the Shadow side lurk in everyone's life. You might not want to advertize these qualities to the world at large but you would be better off if you had admitted them into your awareness and owned them, whatever they are—addictions, infidelity, anger, and jealousy, to name a few. Sometimes roles, brands, and Shadow qualities interface.

To give you an idea of the range of possibility, I am going to describe two individuals caught in the Shadow Side. Both are in the victim role and both have complaining as their brand. Neither of these individuals will admit that they are in the victim role but they both acknowledge that they complain. To show you how engrained they are in their role and brand and how unconscious they are as to what is really going on, I explore the consequences of their actions from a long-term perspective

Uncle Tom is a sarcastically funny guy who always complains. It is hard to see that he is a victim but easy to see that complaining is one of the qualities that he sells to the world, along with sarcasm and nitpicking. When Uncle Tom finally gets that factory manager promotion that he has always wanted, and complained about not getting for ten years, he turns it down because he would have to work longer hours, take on more responsibility, and not be able to go to his lake cottage on weekends. Moreover, if he took the job, his role and what he sells to the world, along with his brand of complaining, would no longer be effective. He would then have to change his brand because it would be invalid for his audience. However, if he turns the job down, he can still complain how long it took for them to offer him the position and make other excuses, like the timing didn't work for him because he is now older. In this case Uncle Tom just transfers his complaints to other issues. He does not really have to change his brand, he just has to adjust it slightly so as to not lose his friends or "market share." We all have friends that fit into similar categories, for whom nothing is ever right or ever good enough. Look around. It could be you! Fear of change as well as fear of the unknown keeps us stuck in old Shadow Side patterns.

Kate is the quintessential victim who doesn't want to work, and so continues to sell her brand of complaining to her family about how sick she is all the time. Her family keeps on buying her brand and supporting her by giving her money. Now Kate is forty-five, single, has never married, and is incapable of ever working, but her parents are now entering another lifespan category—senior citizens. They were negatively affected by the 2008 stock market crash and did not have the affluence on which they used to depend. However, they had created a cripple by giving Kate everything that she wanted. Kate sold complaining, tenacity, and stubbornness to her family because she did not want to grow up; she only wanted to continue being the Victim so she that she could sell her brand of complaining. The cost for playing this role and selling this brand was Kate's life; the payoff was money and never having to work, so she could remain in the role of the sick child. The cost to her parents was enormous. They had to drastically change their lifestyle in their senior years to keep on supporting her—a multigenerational disaster. Clearly, payoff strategies come in many forms and can make the individuals involved feel guilty, disrespected, or inferior. Some of them may also have secondary gain built into them, such as getting attention, feeling sorry, or getting money. Kate may never have understood what she lost because she was caught in unhealthy patterns of her Shadow Side and didn't really have any consciousness about what she was doing or the consequences of what she was doing. Kate's fear of taking responsibility choked her own life force and created an illness. Her survival skills were unhealthy Shadow Side behaviors that took enormous energy to continue sustaining. Those behaviors had been working for Kate for years, so changing them would take a lot of work, which she was not willing to do. Eventually, Kate lost her life to cancer. The story of Kate and her family is tragic. Look around. Stories like this are happening every single day around you—it may even be you. Know that you always have the opportunity to transform your life and move your brand from the Shadow Side to the Healthy Side. It just takes work.

The sixth category is your *compensation factor*. When you come to understand this habitual coping mechanism and are conscious of the patterns that exist within, you will be more aware of when you are off balance in your life.

The seventh category comprises your *desired outcomes*, must be compatible with your soul desires and address the overall purpose of your life. Besides your own individual desires I want you to also address five categories: spiritual, financial, emotional, physical, and environmental with balance as the aspirational goal. Each Soul Transformation Blueprint will be different because each soul journey is original. Your Soul Transformation Blueprint is very important for understanding your life. Any psychologist will tell you that the aspirational goal and the realistic situation will be inconsistent because we live in the human realm and are not perfect.

The following examples will help you clarify which aspects of the seven areas are working for you and which ones are not. It really helps to concretize them by putting them down on paper and comparing them, as Thomas's example demonstrates. As you read through the following example think about your own life, and how you run it and then prepare your own Soul Transformation Blueprint with the template provided at the end of the chapter.

Thomas, the Architect

Thomas is a creative individual who has the capacity for change and growth. He approached his Soul Transformation Blueprint by communing with his Invisible Actor over many weeks and in the process answered many lifelong questions such as: *Who am I? What am I doing? Where am I going? What is my soul purpose?* Professionally his life is going in the direction that he envisioned, but his family life and marriage are lacking artfulness. His wife recently told him that she was unhappy, which was a shock to him, and later in the same week he found out that his sixteen-year-old daughter was caught smoking marijuana at school. Thomas takes responsibility for his part in the decline of their family and home life because he was so focused on developing his business during the day and feeding his Internet porn addiction at night that he had not given his wife or daughter the attention that they needed. He was clearly engaged in his compensation factor of being emotionally unavailable. He even admitted to being so engaged that he did not deal with the maintenance of their home—a leaky roof in the spare bedroom and chipped tile in the upstairs bathroom.

In terms of living his life in balance, Thomas needs to work on all five areas. Spiritually he is connected to his work through his artistic visions. From an environmental perspective, he is building creative, easily affordable homes for young families, using natural and organic materials. Financially he is doing well, but is not putting any attention toward his retirement. Emotionally he feels a bit lost and needs to regain his footing. He needs to put effort toward his marriage, and family life, which could be a place of nurturance for him. He needs to give back to his community by doing some pro bono work, something he hasn't done in ten years. He also needs to go back to the gym, a place he has not been for six months.

Thomas is a good guy, not perfect, but doing the best he can. He needs to realign his priorities and make some different choices. Working through the Soul Transformation Blueprint yourself makes you face your issues. Thomas needs to take a deeper level of responsibility for his life and align with his Soul Transformation Blueprint, so that he can move forward in the direction of his desired outcome and soul purpose.

THOMAS'S SOUL TRANSFORAMTION BLUEPRINT

REALISTIC SITUATION

1) Value Systems: Integrity, consistency and help-fulness—**needs work.**

Steadfastness, Determination, Creativity—**are working**.

2) Roles Thomas Plays: Collaborator, father, lover, son—**needs work.**

Builder and creator—**are working.**

3) What Thomas Sells: Innovation, competency, well-meaningness, artistic design practicality—**are all working.**

4) Thomas's Brand: Creator—**is working.**

5) Thomas's Shadow: Addicted to Internet porn sites; anger issues—**needs work.**

6) Compensation Factor: Emotionally unavailable—**needs work.**

7) Desired Outcomes: Build a successful family—**needs work.**

Build a successful home—**needs work.**

Build a successful business—**is working.**

Give back to the community—
needs work.

To live my life in balance spiritually—**is working**

To live life in balance financially—
not working.

To live life in balance emotionally—
not working.

To live life in balance physically—
not working.

To live my life in balance environmentally—**is working.**

ASPIRATIONAL GOALS

1) Value Systems: Integrity, consistency, helpfulness, steadfastness, determination, creative.

2) Roles Thomas Plays: Builder, collaborator, creator, father, lover, son.

3) What Thomas Sells: Innovation, competency, well-meaningness, Artistic design practicality—are all working.

4) Thomas's Brand: Creator.

5) Thomas's Shadow: To reduce and become more aware of my Shadow Side in all the areas of my life.

6) Compensation Factor: Emotional unavailability in check.

7) Desired Outcomes: Build a successful home, family, and business.

Give back to the community.

To live my life in balance spiritually.

To live life in balance financially.

To live life in balance emotionally.

To live life in balance physically.

To live my life in balance environmentally.

Sally, the Nurse and Mother

Sally is an effervescent, bubbly individual who is dedicated to her children and family. She found the Soul Transformation Blueprint very difficult to work through, taking many months to complete and address the questions: *Who am I? What am I doing?* and *What is my soul purpose?* One of the reasons Sally had great difficulty with this process was that she was overly focused on her role as a mom so that when she became aware how out of touch she was with her husband, she found it shockingly painful. She realized that she had not given her husband any attention for years and knew that she took him for granted. She admitted to not having sex for two years and even though he asked for this intimacy, she just ignored him. Yet when they went out to parties Sally would drink too much and flirt with other men, which in turn increased the tension in their marriage. Facing these Shadow Side issues were agonizing for Sally because she imagined herself to be a great wife, yet the reality of the situation was different. During therapy sessions she kept telling me—*Honestly, I am a good person*—her brand. When I suggested that she and her husband go on an intimate vacation together to try to reconnect, she got very defensive stating that they hadn't done that in years and admitted to being afraid that they would not have anything in common. Even though her children (twelve, fourteen and sixteen) were doing well, she made every possible excuse to not leave them even for a long weekend. Sally was overly dependent on her children, which pushed the entire family unit off balance. Change was not an easy process for Sally because she had a hard time facing her Shadow Side.

In terms of living her life in balance Sally had succeeded in some areas but needed to do some intense work in other areas. She felt that as a couple she and her husband were doing well financially and that she was pulling her weight with her part-time job as a nurse. As for giving back to the community she was always volunteering her services to community outreach programs. Environmentally she felt she was participating by recycling and taking unwanted items to Good Will and the Salvation Army. However, Sally was not building a successful family and home life. She disregarded her husband, the father of her children.

When I brought to her attention the imprint that she was passing onto her children—Dads are not important and that marriages and relationships can be loveless—she was devastated. Besides this issue there were other emotional issues that were repressed, as evidenced by her drinking too much and flirting with other men, which her children had observed on numerous occasions. Spiritually, Sally was feeling empty and admitted that she hadn't been to church since the baptism of her last child. Physically she had not worked out in years and had put on thirty pounds, which certainly did not please her.

Sally is essentially a good person with good values who just got a bit derailed in her approach to life. The Soul Transformation Blueprint was able to illuminate a lot of areas on which she needed to work. In her own time and with psychological treatment Sally was able to bridge the gap between her reality and her illusions. With time she recalibrated her priorities and healed her relationship with her husband. They even went on a vacation that she referred to as their second honeymoon.

SALLY'S SOUL TRANSFORMATION BLUEPRINT

REALISTIC SITUATION

1) Value Systems: Helpful, kind, efficient, competent—**are working.**

Family-oriented, loving, orderly, caring—**needs work.**

2) Roles Sally Play: Caretaker, helper, mother, daughter—**are working.**

Organizer, lover—**needs work.**

3) What Sally Sells: Goodness—**is working.**

4) Sally's Brand: I am a good person—**needs work.**

5) Sally's Shadow: Drinks too much—**needs work.**

Avoids her husband emotionally—**needs work.**

Overly dependent on her children—**needs work.**

6) Compensation Factor: Tries too hard to please everyone—**needs work.**

7) Desired Outcomes: To be appreciated and loved by everyone—**needs work.**

To build a successful home—**needs work.**

To build a successful family—**needs work.**

To build a successful career—**is working.**

To be a great mom—**not working.**

To be a great wife—**not working.**

To grow children that are moral, kind, caring, and compassionate—**needs work.**

To give back to the community—**working.**

To live my life in balance spiritually—**not working.**

To live life in balance financially—**working.**

To live life in balance emotionally—**not working.**

To live life in balance physically—**not working.**

To live my life in balance environmentally—**is working.**

ASPIRATIONAL GOALS

1) **Value Systems:** Helpful, caring, kind, family oriented, orderly, loving, efficient, competent.

2) **Roles Sally Play:** Caretaker, helper, organizer, mother, lover, daughter.

3) **What Sally Sells:** Goodness.

4) **Sally's Brand:** I am a good person!

5) **Sally's Shadow:** To reduce and become more aware of my Shadow Side.

6) **Compensation Factor:** Tries too hard to please everyone.

7) **Desired Outcomes:** To be appreciated and loved by everyone.

To have a successful home, family, and career.

To be a great mom.

To be a great wife.

To grow children that are kind, caring, and compassionate.

To give back to the community.

To live my life in balance spiritually, financially, emotionally, physically, and environmentally.

The Value of the Soul Transformation Blueprint

The value of the Soul Transformation Blueprint is that it brings consistency to inconsistency. It gets you back on track regarding what is really important—keeping your life in balance and in the direction that you want it to go. It is the reality versus illusion perspective. Also aligned with this Soul Transformation Blueprint are the concepts of integrity (what you say you do) and congruency (where your inner and your outer world align). Embodying integrity and congruency is an important part of the process of soul transformation. When you are working through the Soul Transformation Blueprint you need to ask the people around you for help in figuring out where you stand in some of the categories, because it is very hard to see them yourself. Bear in mind that it may also be hard to hear your friends and family tell you things that you did that created negative feelings for you or others. Explore the underlying values that come into play as well as any negative roles that you are using, such as manipulation, power plays, or threats, to get what you want. Be honest about your motives and your responses to other people and events. This is a valuable exercise. When I did this myself I learned a lot more about myself as well as the way that people saw me. Enjoy the process of re-creating your life.

SOUL TRANSFORMATION BLUEPRINT

REALISTIC SITUATION

1) Value Systems:

2) Roles You Play:

3) What You Sell:

5) Your Brand:

4) Your Shadow:

6) Compensation Factor:

7) Desired Outcomes:

SOUL TRANSFORMATION BLUEPRINT

ASPIRATIONAL GOALS

1) Value Systems:

2) Roles You Play:

3) What You Sell:

4) Your Brand:

5) Your Shadow:

6) Compensation Factor:

7) Desired Outcome:

PART III

THE TRANSCENDANT SOUL

CHAPTER 13

CONTINUAL SOUL ENGAGEMENT

ontinual soul engagement is the fifth and final stage of soul transformation. It is a stage of transcendence, a shift in consciousness from engaging illusions to continual soul engagement. When you are in this sacred space, you are beyond illusions and in a new dimension of conceptualizing life because you are free from suffering, desire, and ignorance. At this stage your contextual factors no longer have any impact because you are in alignment with the Divine. Clearly this type of transcendent engagement is difficult to attain fully but it is what we all should all aspire to in one way or another. When you reach this level of enlightenment, as some rare spiritual teachers have, there is no differentiation or separation between the Divine and human realms, only the continual merging of oneness with the universe.

Included in this transcendent space, along with other Divine decrees, are the four Divine truths: truth, love, peace, and right moral and ethical judgment and action. All of these are vital for continual soul engagement because they are equated with the continual creation energy of transcendence. Embedded in the

Divine truths is ancient and universal knowledge that can heal suffering, darkness, and pain on multiple levels—which is why people who reach this realm are considered to be enlightened.

Continual soul engagement is mythically aligned with the hero and heroine's journey because finding the Holy Grail is considered to be one of the highest aspirations—the chalice of kingship. Finding the Holy Grail demonstrates that enormous physical, spiritual, and emotional risks have been taken and that the demands of the journey, though perilous, were accomplished. This archetypal myth of initiation aligns with other spiritual traditions and has as its prize the ability to live life with the highest transformational capacity, which allows one access to the Key of Salvation, the highest level of moral and ethical transcendence. This journey is a lonely one because it moves an individual beyond his or her tribe to another dimension where human perfection and soul development are the victorious prizes. When you have reached this realm, you have left your comfort zone and immersed yourself in the transmutational fires of life and triumphed against all odds. This journey brings with it a deeper understanding of who you are and defines your soul purpose—you have engaged in the adventure and have lived to tell the story. The hero's journey is a continuing journey about the transformation of consciousness that honors the Divine . . . it is soul transformation.

Continual soul engagement can also be examined from a depth psychological perspective. *Individuation*, a concept developed by Carl Jung, refers to this process as the highest level of integration of consciousness with the unconscious. For Jung the ultimate integration of the personality was *wholeness*, resulting from reaching these highest levels, which he describes as a union with the Self, the ultimate achievement of a religious quest. Jung believed that the engagement of a religious quest was crucial for evolving to higher levels of consciousness. Jung's brilliant body of work continually inspires me as I continue the path with my own individuation process. Clearly, without the psychospiritual process of individuation, it is hard to find your authentic-soul centered Self in the world.

Continual soul engagement is not generally considered to be a life goal in Western culture. Most individuals in this society look at the focus of life as a *pattern of exchange* rather than a *progression of soul*. By *pattern of exchange* I mean the acquiring of things. There are two layers to this exchange. The first layer is a pattern of exchange that involves *getting things* by going to school, going to work, buying a home, having a family, so that you can eventually have a successful retirement. Sometimes the spiritual is addressed, but not in all cases. A lot of these exchange patterns are attached to our contextual factors and Western views of life, including the one from which I write. However, these unconscious engraved exchange patterns limit our capacity to answer two existential questions: *Who am I?* and *What is my soul purpose?* The exchange patterns are unconscious processes in the Western mind, which is why I believe that so many people struggle to find answers to them. The second layer has to do with an individual getting his or her *needs met*. When you struggle to get anything, as in a pattern of exchange, even if it is truth, peace, love, or right judgment and action, you are in an illusion. For example, how many people do you know who are trying to get love? Many I presume. If you try to get love, you suffer because the problem of getting love is complex. How can you get love when you didn't get any love in your family? If your contextual factors have an unhealthy love pattern within them then you want something that you never had, you have an illusion about it, know it is possible and desperately desire it but you have no imprint to get it. If you relate to this, you need to rework your psychological structure. People who do not have healthy love imprints usually feel unloved, unworthy, needy, and are angry as adults. So if this type of individual tries to get love, all they get is suffering because of the lack of healthy exchange patterning.

Progression of soul is all about increasing your level of consciousness and connecting to your soul. If you shift your stance and perspective, for example, from *getting* love to *being love,* then you can shift your energy and your focus and increase the possibility of creating a loving experience because your inner world mirrors your outer world. These *being* stances must exist within you, because your inner world creates your outer world and are part of the soul progression process. If you come from a place of *being*, you take control, that is, *soul control* of your life. What you need to understand is that all *getting* gets you is suffering in the illusion, whereas *being*, a pattern of nonattachment, moves you toward the divine realm, which takes you to the stance of soul transformation. It is my understanding and perspective that soul transformation is the ultimate purpose of life in the human realm, as evidenced by the mythic, archetypal, psychological, and spiritual traditions.

Spiritual teachers of many traditions—Christian, Buddhist, Hindu, Kabala, Muslim, and Sufism—will bring to your attention, in their own unique way, that the true purpose of life is not about a pattern of exchange but the progression of soul. Being on a soul journey has the tremendous benefit of increasing your consciousness and you're your understanding of life, leading you along an authentic soul-centered path. We must all awaken from the illusion that we are separate, and own that we are one with the Divine. I believe that our soul purpose is to connect to the energy of the Divine and move beyond suffering so that we can experience the enlightened grandeur of the Universe.

When you approach life from the perspective of soul transformation you will find yourself asking questions such as:

1. What is the bigger picture?

2. How can I make a shift in my consciousness?

3. How can I see through the illusion?

4. What are the lessons that I need to learn from this situation?

If your boyfriend leaves you for another woman and in the process compromises your financial situation, perhaps its time to consider the bigger picture of owning your own feminine power, financially, emotionally, and spiritually, so that no matter what happens in your life, you will be able to handle it—any disaster, trauma, or curveball. The larger purpose of your story can then become clear to you: The dysfunctional relationship with your boyfriend caused you to become more responsible for your life, and you need not depend on him, or anyone else, to save you. This attitude, though difficult for most individuals to engage, keeps you focused in the *here and now* . . . living life fully in a sacred way. It also takes you away from engaging in the Shadow Side roles of Victim, Narcissist, or Dissasociate, to name a few. When you approach life as a continual shifting of consciousness, you move into the Divine flow of life rather than into a pattern of exchange.

Let's say that you fell off a ladder at work and were no longer able to function in your capacity as a roofer. Perhaps the Divine is opening you up to retool, to work at a job that is less dangerous and aligned with some new capabilities, perhaps some that you have not yet developed. I knew a university professor who was fighting to keep her teaching job, while the Divine was guiding her to quit her job and engage her soul journey to become a shaman and spiritual teacher—which she eventually did and became very successful. Remember, there are no such things as accidents, only the Divine moving you to a new level of potentiality.

You may discover your sense of soul from experiences or events that were expected, unexpected, or chosen. These experiences allow the Invisible Actor to vivify within you and potentially change the direction of your life. However, even though life events may precipitate change, you can also take control and engage in specific psychological and spiritual processes that can continually shift you toward being a better individual by gradually realizing a higher level of existence.

Unless you are open to unique life experiences, to interesting mentors, a specific spiritual practice, or are involved with different cultures, you will remain fairly narrow in your perception of life and will likely engage in the illusions around you. The question you need to answer is this: *Is this the way that I wish to live my life?* Some individuals are content with this level of existence, but if you are drawn to a different approach and want to move toward eternal truths rather than clinging to illusions, then you must partake purposefully in practices that foster such a movement—practices such as prayer, spiritual rituals, meditation, and psychological development that embraces dream work, transformational symbols, images and synchronicities to give you more opportunities with which to engage soul. Being proactive engages soul energy and helps you to loosen some of the shackles that bind your movement. Living with soul does not mean that you shouldn't be successful, but that you are able to blend both perspectives into your life: the spiritual and the material.

In this book I have provided you with multiple ways to engage your soul, both psychologically and spiritually. The psychological process is important because it assists you in the management of your daily life and all your relationships. But in order to transform to the highest level, you need to go to the level of soul. Soul transformation approaches can cleanse and untangle complex psychological and spiritual issues, even those that are family and lineage based. They also have the capacity to wash away the negative imprints engrained in our inner child. To recap the four soul transformation approaches in the book include:

1. The Five stages of Soul Transformation
2. The Trinity Model
3. The Soul Transformation Process
4. The Soul Transformation Blueprint

Each approach assists you to become more conscious of the inner and outer forces that shape your life. Knowing yourself is an amazing life goal that allows you to make smarter more conscious choices. Using the combination of philosophical perspectives, psychological tools along with the soul transformation approaches provided in this book will help you get back on track to live your life on the Healthy Side. In addition, when you are on a soul-inspired journey, your relationship to your physical body will have a different meaning. The more embodied you are, the more ensouled you are, which in turn will increase your consciousness level. It is my perspective that both the psychological and spiritual disciplines are necessary to keep any individual in balance. I once knew an extraordinarily brilliant and spiritual man who was in denial of his psychological state and refused to get help for his issues because he thought he was beyond "all that." Instead he marginalized himself and cut off his true potentiality because of a layer of shame that he did not want to deal with, as well as his *holier-than-thou* attitude, a shadowland default position. Even though he was one of the most brilliant individuals that I have ever encountered, he was incapable of living in the world in a functional manner. My point is that without a strong psychological grounding, your spirituality may take you toward Shadow Side stances, and you may not even realize it—no matter how enormous your intelligence and spiritual understanding.

The writing of this book was an intense experience for me, certainly part of my own individuation process, my heroine's journey, and my spiritual quest fueled by the archetype of transformation that enlivens the flesh, blood, and bones of my earthly existence. I am psychologically and spiritually aligned with my career as a clinical psychologist as well as with my soul purpose. The creation process of this book pushed me to find an accessible way to discuss some very difficult and highly charged spiritual perspectives. You need to choose your own path, one that aligns with your unique journey as well as the level of soul transformation that you wish to attain.

Embrace the archetype of transformation, a collective pattern that facilitates your passage through the continually shifting processes of life that can transform your imprinted patterns of limitation. Use the Trinity Model, the Soul Transformation Process, and the Soul Transformation Blueprint as tools to guide you in the process of increasing your consciousness level. Engage a mentor, spiritual teacher, or psychologist to gently support and energize your efforts.

The process of Soul Transformation honors the sacred image of self and aligns with the Invisible Actor. Living an authentic soul-centered journey of self-discovery and working toward achieving the highest levels is the journey of soul transformation. Utilize the psychospiritual Trinity Model to grow up the Healthy and Divine Sides and shrink the Shadow Side. Dismantle your illusions so that you can move through life with more clarity and conscious vision. My deepest wish is that you engage the Invisible Actor within, bringing consciousness to the illusions that surround you, so that you can live your life with luminous sparkle and awe as you move forward along the path of soul transformation.

WHO AM I?

A bright, shiny light in the world that facilitates transformation!

WHAT IS MY SOUL PURPOSE?

To transform myself and others!

REFERENCES

Berry, P. (1982). *Echo's subtle body.* Dallas, TX: Spring Publications.

Corbett, L. (1996). *The religious function of the psyche.* New York: Routledge.

Edinger, E. (1972). *Ego and archetype.* Boston: Shambhala Publications.

Edinger, E. (1994). *The eternal drama: The inner meaning of Greek mythology.* Boston: Shambhala Publications.

Edinger, E. (2002). *Science of soul.* Toronto: Inner City Books.

Green, L. (1995). *The astrology of fate.* York Beach, ME: Samuel Weiser.

Haule, J. (1999). *Perils of the soul.* York Beach, ME: Samuel Weiser.

Hillman, J. (1975). *Re-visioning psychology.* New York: HarperPerennial.

Hillman, J. (1979). *The dream and the underworld.* New York: HarperPerennial.

Hillman, J. (1996). *The soul's code.* New York: Random House.

Hillman, J. (1999). *The force of character.* New York: Ballantine Books.

Hollis, J. (1996). *Swamplands of the soul.* Toronto: Inner City Books.

Jacoby, M. (1985). *Individuation and narcissism.* New York: Routledge.

Jaffe, L. (1999). *Celebrating soul.* Toronto: Inner City Books.

Jung, C. G. (1950). Depth psychology (R. F. C. Hull, Trans.). In H. Read et al.

(Series Eds.), *The collected works of C. G. Jung. Vol. 18, The symbolic life* (pp. 477-486). Princeton, NJ: Princeton University Press. (Original work published 1948)

Jung, C. G. (1953). Psychology and alchemy (R. F. C. Hull, Trans.). In H. Read et al. (Series Eds.), *The collected works of C. G. Jung. Vol. 12 Introduction to the religious and psychological problems of alchemy* (pp. 1-38). Princeton, NJ: Princeton University Press.

Jung, C. G. (1954). The development of personality (R. F. C. Hull, Trans.). In H. Read et al. (Series Eds.), *The collected works of C.G.Jung. Vol.17, The development of personality* (pp. 165-186). New York: Pantheon Books. (Original work published 1934)

Jung, C. G. (1958). Psychology and religion (R. F. C. Hull, Trans.). In H. Read et al. (Series Eds.), *The collected words of C. G. Jung. Vol. 11 Psychology and religion: East and West* (pp. 5-111). Princeton, NJ: Princeton University Press. (Original work published 1937)

Jung, C. G. (1958). A psychological approach to the dogma of the trinity (R.F.C. Hull, Trans.). In H. Read et al. (Series Eds.), *The collected works of C. G. Jung. Vol. 11 psychology and religion: east and west* (pp. 107-200). Princeton, NJ: Princeton University Press. (Original work published 1948)

Jung, C. G. (1960) The spirit in man, art, and literature (R.F.C. Hull, Trans.). In H. Read et al. (Series Eds.), *The collected works of C.G. Jung. Vol.15. Psychology and literature* (pp. 84-108). New York: Princeton University Press. (Original work published in 1950)

Jung, C. G. (1960). Concept of the collective unconscious (R. F. C. Hull, Trans.). In H. Read et al. (Series Eds.), *The collected works of C.G. Jung*. Vol. 9, Part 1 *The archetypes and the collective unconscious* (pp. 42-53). New York: Pantheon Books. (Original work published1954)

Jung, C. G. (1960). The transcendent function (R .F. C. Hull, Trans.). In H. Read et al. (Series Eds.), *The collected works of C. G. Jung, Vol. 8 The structure and dynamics of the psyche* (pp. 67-91). New York: Pantheon Books. (Original work published 1958)

Jung, C. G. (1989). *Memories, dreams, reflections*. New York: Vintage Books.

Jung, C. G. (1990). *The undiscovered self*. Princeton, NJ: Princeton University Press.

Kalsched, D. (1996). *The innerworld of trauma*. London: Routledge.

Levine, P. (1997). *Walking the tiger – healing trauma*. Berkeley: North Atlantic Books.

Mattoon, M. (1981). *Jungian psychology in perspective*. New York: Free Press.

Moore, T. (1992). *Care of the soul*. New York: Harper Collins.

Otto, R. (1923). *The idea of the holy*. London: Oxford University Press.

Papalia, D., Olds, S., & Feldman, R., (2001). *Human diversity*. New York: McGraw Hill.

Raff, J. (2000). *Jung and the alchemical imagination*. York Beach, ME: Nicolas-Hays.

Romanyshyn, R. (1989). *Technology as symptom and dream*. New York: Routledge.

Romanyshyn, R. (1991). Complex knowing: Toward a psychological hermeneutics. *Humanistic Psychologist, 19*(1), 10-29.

Romanyshyn, R. (2002). *Ways of the heart.* Pittsburgh: Trivium Publications.

Roob, A. (2001). *Alchemy and mysticism.* New York: Taschen.

Sardello, R. (2004). *Facing the world with soul.* Great Barrington, MA: Lindesfarne.

Schimmel, A. (1993). *The mystery of numbers.* New York: Oxford University Press.

Schwartz-Salant, N. (1982*). Narcissism and character transformation.* Toronto: Inner City Books.

Schwartz-Salant, N. (1995). *Jung in alchemy.* New York: Routledge.

Schwartz-Salant, N. (1998). *The mystery of human relationship.* New York: Routledge.

Singer, J. (1972). *Boundaries of the soul.* New York: Double Day.

Slattery, D. (2000a). Narcissus, Echo, and irony's resonance. In *Psychology at the threshold* (pp. 67-83). Carpinteria, CA: Pacifica Graduate Institute.

Slattery, D. (2000b, February). The soul's sounding. *The Salt Journal. 2*(2), pp. 20-36.

Slattery, D. (2000c). *The wounded body: Remembering the markings of flesh.* Albany, NY: State University of New York Press.

Stein, M. (1997). *Jungian analysis.* La Salle, IL: Open Court.

Stein, M. (1998). *Jung's map of the soul.* La Salle, IL: Open Court.

12503482R00103

Made in the USA
Charleston, SC
09 May 2012